# Success

## 10 Minute Tests

# Maths

### age 9–10 · level 3–5

Paul Broadbent

# Sample page

topic being covered

test number for quick reference

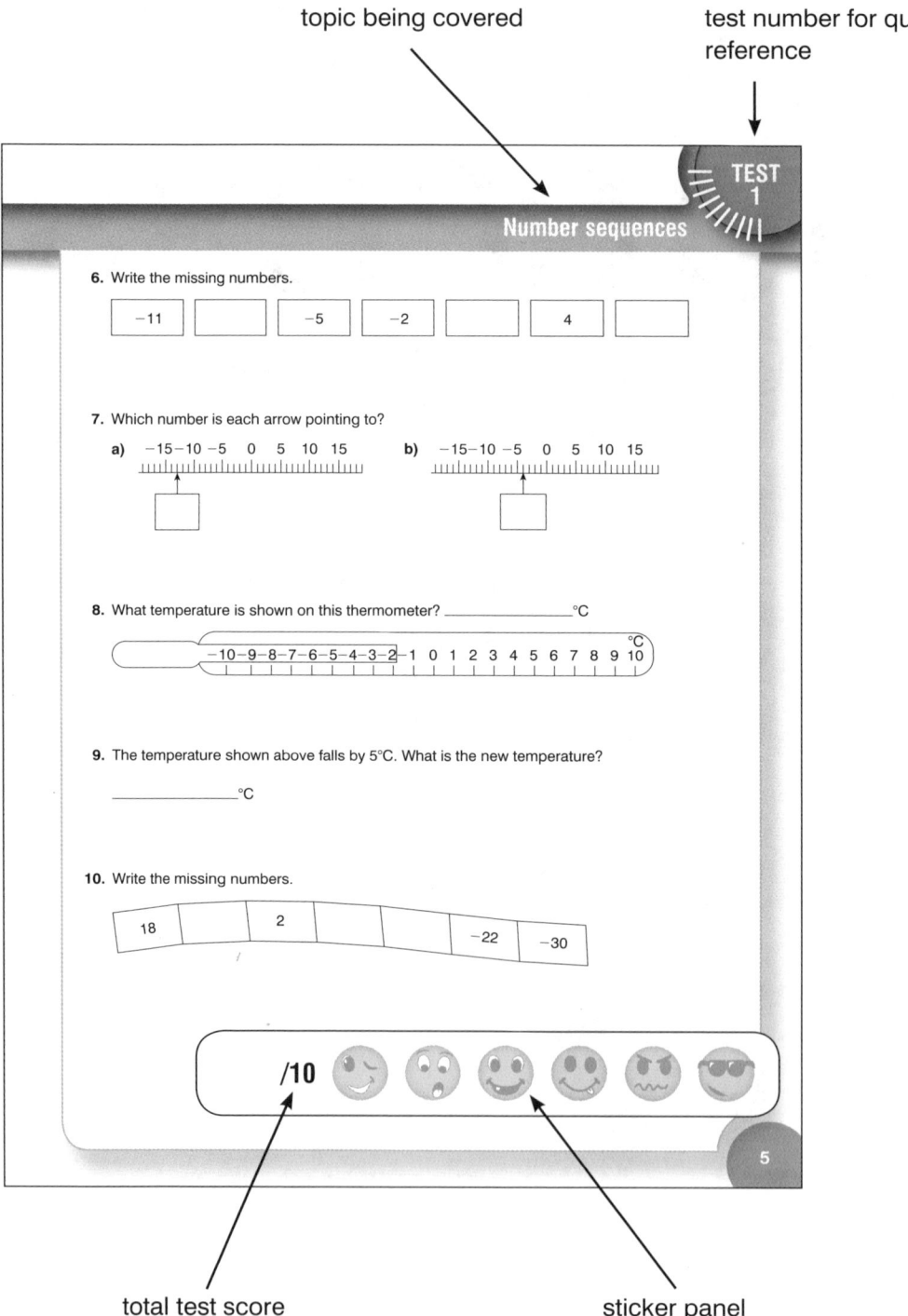

**TEST 1**

Number sequences

**6.** Write the missing numbers.

| −11 | | −5 | −2 | | 4 | |

**7.** Which number is each arrow pointing to?

a)  −15 −10 −5   0   5   10   15

b)  −15 −10 −5   0   5   10   15

**8.** What temperature is shown on this thermometer? _____ °C

−10 −9 −8 −7 −6 −5 −4 −3 −2 −1 0 1 2 3 4 5 6 7 8 9 10 °C

**9.** The temperature shown above falls by 5°C. What is the new temperature?

_____ °C

**10.** Write the missing numbers.

| 18 | | 2 | | | −22 | −30 |

/10

5

total test score

sticker panel

# Contents

## Number sequences

**1.** Write the next three numbers in this sequence.

| 63 | 74 | 85 | 96 | | | |
|----|----|----|----|--|--|--|

**2.** Write the missing numbers.

| 14 | | 2 | −4 | −10 | | |
|----|--|---|----|-----|--|--|

**3.** Which number is each arrow pointing to?

**a)**   −15 −10 −5   0   5   10   15

**b)**   −15 −10 −5   0   5   10   15

**4.** What temperature is shown on this thermometer? _____°C

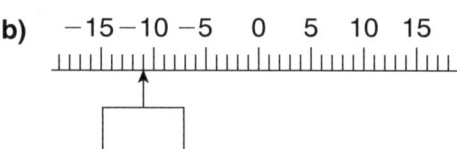

°C
−10 −9 −8 −7 −6 −5 −4 −3 −2 −1 0 1 2 3 4 5 6 7 8 9 10

**5.** The temperature shown above rises by 6°C. What is the new temperature?

_____°C

6. Write the missing numbers.

| −11 | | −5 | −2 | | 4 | |

7. Which number is each arrow pointing to?

a)  −15 −10 −5  0  5  10  15

b)  −15 −10 −5  0  5  10  15

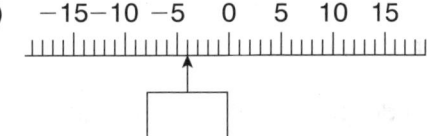

8. What temperature is shown on this thermometer? _____°C

°C
−10 −9 −8 −7 −6 −5 −4 −3 −2 −1 0 1 2 3 4 5 6 7 8 9 10

9. The temperature shown above falls by 5°C. What is the new temperature?

_____°C

10. Write the missing numbers.

| 18 | | 2 | | | −22 | −30 |

/10

## Decimals

**1.** Draw lines to match the decimals to the fractions.

 6.45
 6.5
 4.65
 5.6
 6.54

$6\frac{5}{10}$     $4\frac{65}{100}$     $6\frac{45}{100}$     $6\frac{54}{100}$     $5\frac{6}{10}$

**2.** Write the decimals on this number line.

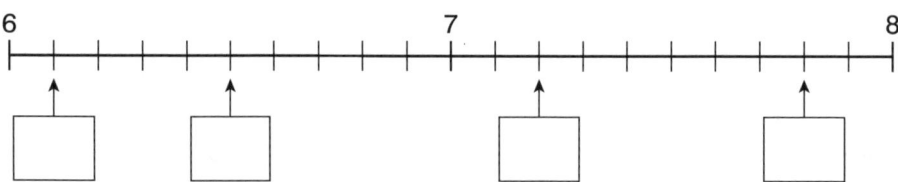

**3.** Write these fractions as decimals.

a) $\frac{34}{100}$ →  ☐     b) $\frac{19}{100}$ →  ☐     c) $\frac{7}{100}$ →  ☐

**4.** Change these decimals to hundredths.

a) 0.51 →  ☐     b) 0.92 →  ☐     c) 0.08 →  ☐

**5.** Rearrange each of these to make a decimal number as close to 4 as possible.

a)  ⑧ ③ ④ ·

b) ⑤ ① · ②

c)  ⑨ ④ ② ·

**6.** Write the decimals on this number line.

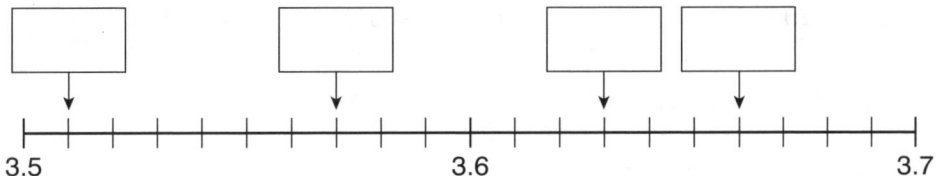

3.5          3.6          3.7

**7.** Write the value of the circled digits as tenths or hundredths.

a) 8.⑨2 → [　　　] 　　b) 13. 1⑧ → [　　　] 　　c) 10.⓪5 → [　　　]

**8.** Write these as decimals.

a) $\frac{1}{100}$ → _____ 　　b) $\frac{21}{100}$ → _____ 　　c) $\frac{90}{100}$ → _____

**9.** Write this as a decimal number:

$400 + 80 + 6 + \frac{7}{10} + \frac{9}{100} =$ _____

**10.** Change these decimals to whole numbers and hundredths.

a) 6.24 → _____ 　　b) 3.21 → _____ 　　c) 7.55 → _____

/10

## Ordering numbers

**1.** Write the sign $<$ or $>$ for each pair of numbers.

   **a)** 20 056 _____ 20 506            **b)** 39 989 _____ 39 898

**2.** Circle the largest number in each pair.

   **a)** 745.5            745.09

   **b)** 36.85            36.58

   **c)** 1207.14         1270.03

**3.** Write these numbers in order, starting with the smallest.

   ( 29 945 )    ( 20 886 )    ( 29 906 )    ( 20 905 )    ( 20 868 )

_____

**4.** Tick the smallest amount in this set.

   35.78 kg ☐     30.19 kg ☐     35.8 kg ☐     30.3 kg ☐     30.47 kg ☐

**5.** Write $<$, $>$ or $=$ between each pair of decimals.

   **a)** 0.01 _____ 0.11    **b)** 0.40 _____ 0.4    **c)** 0.65 _____ 0.56

**6.** These temperatures should be in order, starting with the lowest temperature.
Colour the two temperatures that have been swapped.

**7.** Write these lengths in order, starting with the smallest.

( 37.45 m )     ( 38.33 m )     ( 37.91 m )     ( 38.3 m )     ( 37.5 m )

_____

**8.** These are the costs of 5 train tickets. Write the prices in order, starting with the most expensive.

£38.70

£31.29

£74.88

£40.05

£60.90

_____

**9.** Write the number that is halfway between each pair.

**a)**  5000 _____ 10 000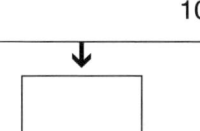

**b)**  0 _____ 50 000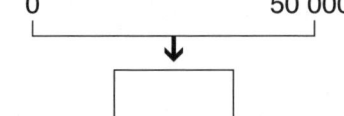

**10.** Write these temperatures in order, starting with the lowest.

−17°C          3°C          0°C          −19°C          −11°C          −20°C

_____

/10

**1.** Draw lines to join these numbers to the nearest 10.

| 6535 | 6575 | 6548 | 6556 | 6573 |

 6530   6540   6550   6560   6570  6580

**2.** Round these numbers to the nearest 100.

**a)** 6869 → _____   **b)** 8055 → _____   **c)** 9344 → _____

**3.** Round these numbers to the nearest pound.

**a)** £18.48 → _____   **b)** £27.52 → _____   **c)** £49.61 → _____

**4.** Write two decimal numbers that would round to 12 to the nearest whole number.

☐ and ☐

**5.** Round each of these to the nearest 100 g.

**a)** **b)** 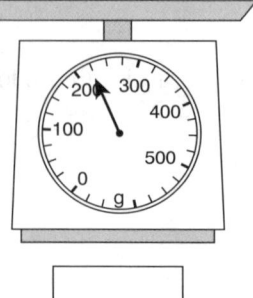 **c)**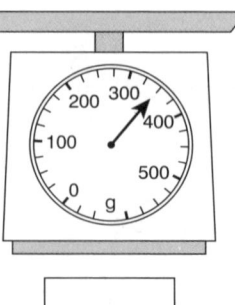

**6.** Estimate how much liquid is in this jug.

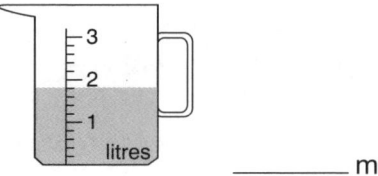

_____ ml

**7.** Circle the number that is nearest to the correct answer for each of these.

**a)** 144 + 262 =     350     400     450

**b)** 352 − 147 =     200     250     300

**8.** Round each number in these calculations to the nearest 10 to give an approximate answer.

**a)** 438 + 327 ➔ _____

**b)** 902 − 578 ➔ _____

**9.** Draw lines to join these decimals to the nearest whole number.

52.83          52.08          55.19          53.51

51          52          53          54          55          56

**10.** Approximately how many hours are there in February in a leap year? Circle the correct range.

100–200 hours          300–400 hours          600–700 hours          800–900 hours

/10

## Fractions, decimals and percentages

**1.** Write these as improper fractions.

a)

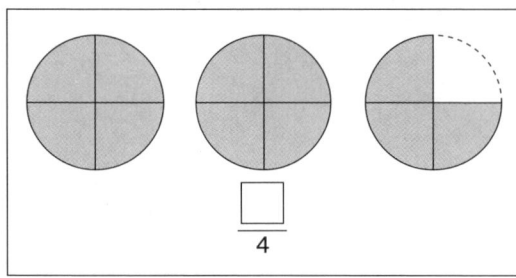

$\frac{\Box}{4}$

b)

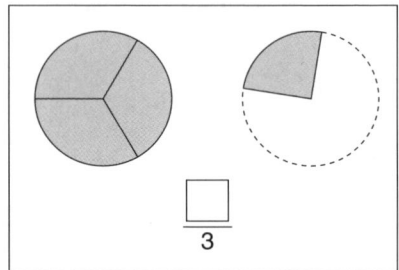

$\frac{\Box}{3}$

**2.** Change these improper fractions to whole numbers and fractions.

a)  $\frac{9}{2}$ = _____

b)  $\frac{15}{4}$ = _____

c)  $\frac{18}{5}$ = _____

d)  $\frac{20}{3}$ = _____

**3.** Complete this table.

| Fractions | Decimals | Percentages |
|---|---|---|
| $\frac{1}{2}$ |  | 50% |
|  | 0.2 |  |
|  |  | 75% |
| $\frac{3}{10}$ |  |  |

**4.** Write the percentage that is shaded.

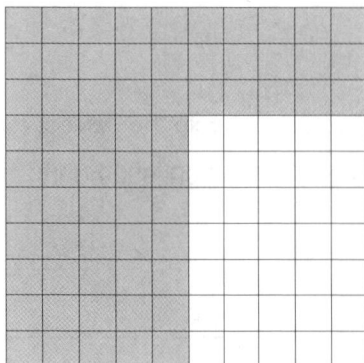

_____%

**5.** Write these fractions as percentages.

a)  $\frac{35}{100}$ = _____

b)  $\frac{1}{4}$ = _____

c)  $\frac{40}{50}$ = _____

# Fractions, decimals and percentages

**6.** Colour these scales to show each percentage.

**a)**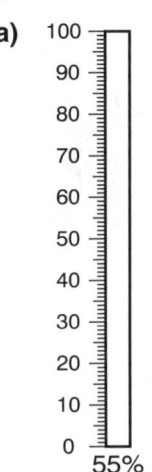
55%

**b)**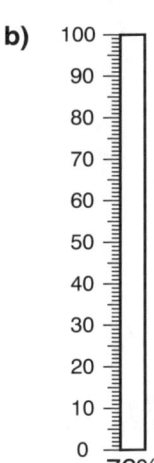
76%

**7.** Draw lines to join the matching fractions, decimals and percentages.

| $\frac{1}{5}$ | $\frac{3}{10}$ | $\frac{45}{100}$ | $\frac{4}{5}$ |

| 0.3 | 0.2 | 0.8 | 0.45 |

| 80% | 45% | 30% | 20% |

**8.** Write these percentages as fractions.

**a)** $90\% = \dfrac{\Box}{\Box}$

**b)** $5\% = \dfrac{\Box}{\Box}$

**c)** $60\% = \dfrac{\Box}{\Box}$

**9.** Use > or < to complete these.

**a)** 0.8 _____ 8%

**b)** 0.2 _____ 50%

**c)** 0.25 _____ 75%

**10.** Change these to improper fractions.

**a)** $4\frac{3}{4} \rightarrow \dfrac{\Box}{\Box}$

**b)** $2\frac{1}{2} \rightarrow \dfrac{\Box}{\Box}$

**c)** $5\frac{2}{3} \rightarrow \dfrac{\Box}{\Box}$

**/10**

## Equivalent fractions

**1.** Write each fraction shaded in two ways.

a)
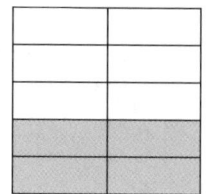

$$\frac{\square}{\square} = \frac{\square}{\square}$$

b)
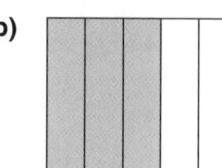
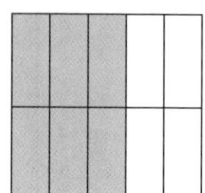

$$\frac{\square}{\square} = \frac{\square}{\square}$$

**2.** Cross out the fraction that is not equivalent.

a)
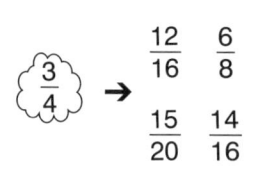

$$\frac{3}{4} \rightarrow \quad \frac{12}{16} \quad \frac{6}{8}$$
$$\frac{15}{20} \quad \frac{14}{16}$$

b)
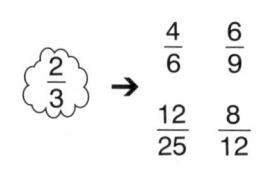

$$\frac{2}{3} \rightarrow \quad \frac{4}{6} \quad \frac{6}{9}$$
$$\frac{12}{25} \quad \frac{8}{12}$$

**3.** Complete this equivalent fraction chain.

$$\frac{2}{5} = \frac{4}{\square} = \frac{\square}{15} = \frac{8}{\square} = \frac{\square}{25}$$

**4.** Write the fraction shaded, using the smallest possible denominator.

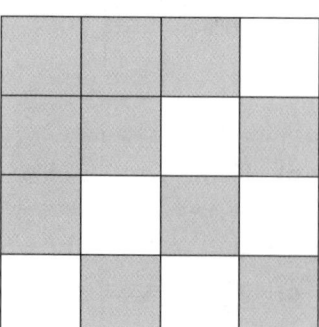

_____

**5.** Complete these equivalent fractions.

a)
$$\frac{3}{10} = \frac{\square}{50}$$

b)
$$\frac{5}{6} = \frac{15}{\square}$$

c)
$$\frac{2}{3} = \frac{40}{\square}$$

**6.** Shade $\frac{2}{3}$ of this circle.

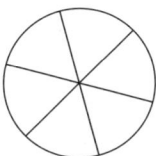

**7.** Write the equivalent fraction shaded on this shape.

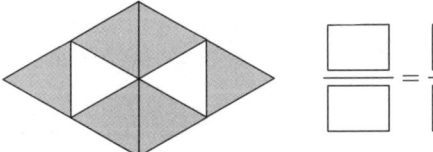

$$\frac{\square}{\square} = \frac{\square}{\square}$$

**8.** Complete this equivalent fraction chain.

$$\frac{5}{8} = \frac{\square}{16} = \frac{15}{\square} = \frac{\square}{32} = \frac{25}{\square}$$

**9.** Simplify each fraction so that you have the smallest possible denominator.

**a)**  $\frac{6}{15} = \frac{\square}{\square}$

**b)**  $\frac{25}{100} = \frac{\square}{\square}$

**c)**  $\frac{14}{16} = \frac{\square}{\square}$

**10.** Write 4 different fractions that are equivalent to $\frac{3}{5}$.

$$\frac{\square}{\square} \quad \frac{\square}{\square} \quad \frac{\square}{\square} \quad \frac{\square}{\square}$$

**/10**

## Ratio and proportion

Colour these tile patterns to match the ratios.

**1.** The ratio of red to blue is 1 to every 3.

**2.** The ratio of green to yellow is 1 to every 4.

**3.** The ratio of black to white is 3 to every 5.

**4.** In a cake recipe, 25 g of cherries is needed for every 100 g of raisins. What weight of cherries is needed for a cake that has 800 g of raisins? _____

**5.** What proportion of this grid is shaded? Give your answer as a fraction.

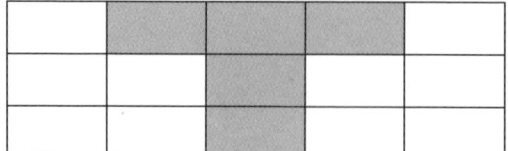

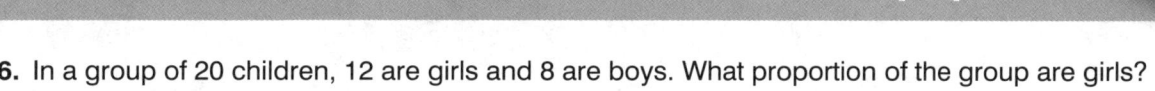
**6.** In a group of 20 children, 12 are girls and 8 are boys. What proportion of the group are girls?

**7.** This is a recipe for 6 people. Write out the ingredients so that it is for 2 people.

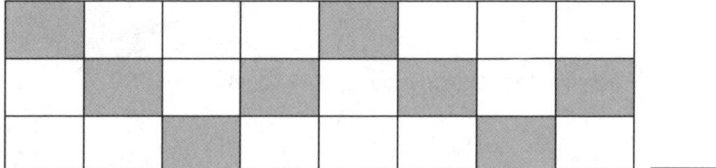

| Fish Pie (for 6 people) | Fish Pie (for 2 people) |
|---|---|
| 600 g fish | _____ fish |
| 1.5 kg potatoes | _____ potatoes |
| 300 g peas | _____ peas |
| 240 g cheese | _____ cheese |
| 120 g butter | _____ butter |
| 180 ml milk | _____ milk |

**8.** What is the ratio of grey to white tiles?

_____

**9.** In a book of 40 pages, 2 out of every 5 of the pages have a picture on them. How many pages have a picture?

_____

**10.** 12 red beads and 16 white beads are kept in a bag. What is the ratio of red to white beads?

_____

/10

## Multiplication and division facts

**1.** Write the missing numbers.

    **a)** $7 \times$ _____ $= 56$      **b)** _____ $\times 9 = 54$      **c)** $4 \times$ _____ $= 32$

**2.** Complete these grids.

    **a)**

| × | 7 | 9 | 6 |
|---|---|---|---|
| 8 | | | |
| 7 | | | |
| 4 | | | |

    **b)**

| × | 10 | 11 | 12 |
|---|----|----|----|
| 8 | | | |
| 9 | | | |
| 10 | | | |

**3.** Answer these.

    **a)** $27 \div 3 =$ _____    **b)** $42 \div 6 =$ _____    **c)** $56 \div 7 =$ _____

**4.** Which two numbers less than 50 can be divided exactly by 2, 3, 4, 6, 8 and 12?

    _____    _____

**5.** Draw lines to join each division to its matching remainder.

| $25 \div 3$ | $44 \div 5$ | $68 \div 9$ | $51 \div 8$ | $44 \div 6$ |

 1    2    3    4    5

**6.** Write two different multiplications for each answer. Do not use the number 1, and all four numbers you use must be different.

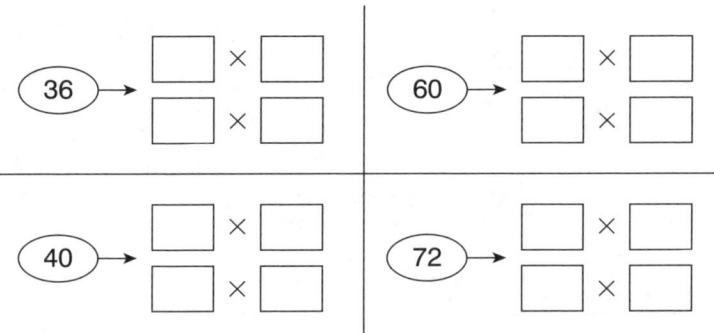

36 →  □ × □
     □ × □

60 →  □ × □
     □ × □

40 →  □ × □
     □ × □

72 →  □ × □
     □ × □

**7.** Complete these grids.

**a)**

| × | 9 | | 6 |
|---|---|---|---|
| 3 | | | |
| 8 | | 40 | |
| | | | 42 |

**b)**

| × | 7 | 4 | |
|---|---|---|---|
| 8 | | | 64 |
| | | 36 | |
| | | | 24 |

**8.** Write the missing numbers.

**a)** 30 × _____ = 180   **b)** _____ × 4 = 200   **c)** 50 × _____ = 350

**9.** I'm thinking of a number. If I divide it by 6 and then add 2 the answer is 7.
What is my number?

_____

**10.** I'm thinking of a number. If I multiply it by 8 and then subtract 2 the answer is 30.
What is my number?

_____

/10

# Factors and multiples

**1.** Write the factors of these numbers in order.

   **a)** 32 → | 1, 2, |

   **b)** 20 → | |

   **c)** 25 → | |

   **d)** 55 → | |

**2.** Answer these.

   **a)** The 5th multiple of 4 is … _____

   **b)** The 6th multiple of 3 is … _____

   **c)** The 4th multiple of 9 is … _____

**3.** Write the three smallest numbers that will fit into the centre shaded part of each Venn diagram.

   **a)**
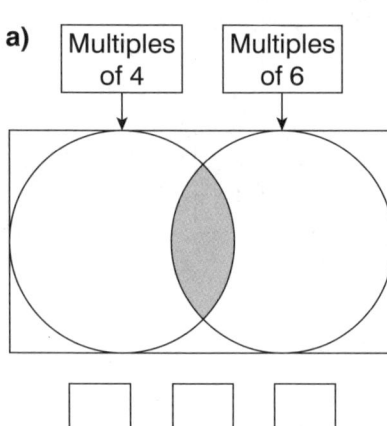

   **b)**
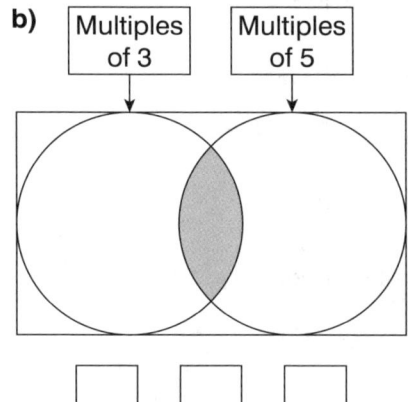

**4.** Write the factors of these numbers in pairs.

   **a)** 28 → (1, 28) _____

   **b)** 45 → _____

   **c)** 40 → _____

   **d)** 24 → _____

**5.** 3 is a factor of 123. Tick the correct answer.

   True ☐     False ☐

Use this set of numbers to answer questions 6–8.

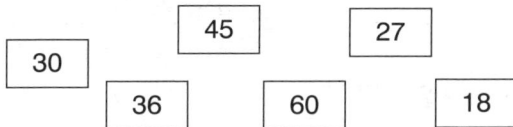

45    27

30

36    60    18

**6.** Which three numbers are multiples of both 3 and 5?

_____    _____    _____

**7.** Which two numbers are multiples of 9, but not multiples of 6?

_____    _____

**8.** Which number is a multiple of 2, 3, 4, 5, 6 and 10?

_____

**9.** Circle the correct answer.

**a)**

A common multiple of 5 and 7 is:

70    60    50    40

**b)**

A common multiple of 3 and 8 is:

16    27    48    56

**10.** 4 is a factor of 98. Tick the correct answer.

True ☐        False ☐

/10

1. Answer these.

   **a)** 108 + 53 = _____   **b)** 125 + 91 = _____   **c)** 146 + 72 = _____

2. Four pairs of these numbers each total 5000. Write the pairs.

   **a)** _____ and _____          **b)** _____ and _____

   **c)** _____ and _____          **d)** _____ and _____

3. Answer these.

   **a)**    1 4 7        **b)**    2 0 9        **c)**    2 3 8        **d)**    3 6 4
          + 1 6 4              + 1 5 8              + 1 8 5              + 2 7 7
          _____              _____              _____              _____

          _____              _____              _____              _____

4. What is the perimeter of this shape? _____

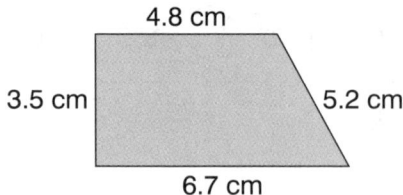

   4.8 cm

   3.5 cm          5.2 cm

   6.7 cm

5. Add each row and column to find the total in the bottom right-hand corner.

| 7.2 | 9.1 | |
|-----|-----|---|
| 6.4 | 8.9 | |
| | | |

**6.** Answer these.

a)
```
  4 1 0 5
+ 2 6 3 9
---------
```

b)
```
  7 6 8 2
+ 1 5 0 8
---------
```

c)
```
  3 8 5 7
+ 4 7 9 4
---------
```

**7.** Sam goes shopping and spends £37.45 on a pair of trainers and £18.99 on a tracksuit. How much does he spend in total?

£_____._____

**8.** Write the missing digits.

a)
```
  □ 3 1 5
+ 1 5 □ 2
---------
  9 8 7 7
```

b)
```
  4 8 2 9
+ 3 □ 5 □
---------
  7 9 8 1
```

c)
```
  4 □ 2 9
+ 2 7 □ 3
---------
  7 0 2 2
```

**9.** Draw lines to join pairs of numbers that total £30

£18.75    £11.25    £10.25    £15.85

£12.55    £19.75    £14.15    £17.45

**10.** Write the missing digits.

| 3 | | 9 | + | 7 | | = | 4 | 2 | 5 |

/10

## Subtraction

**1.** Draw lines to join pairs with a difference of 88.

**2.** Answer these.

a)
```
  1 7 4
−   4 9
───────
```

b)
```
  3 0 8
−   6 2
───────
```

c)
```
  4 1 6
−   5 8
───────
```

**3.** Write the change from £10 for each of these.

a) £3.58

b) £8.27

c) £6.09

**4.** Write the missing digits.

a)
```
  3 8 1
− 1 □ 9
───────
  2 3 □
```

b)
```
  4 □ 8
− □ 9 3
───────
  1 8 5
```

c)
```
  6 0 4
− 3 □ 5
───────
  □ 2 □
```

**5.** I'm thinking of a number. If I subtract 255 from it, the answer is 89.
What number am I thinking of?

_____

This diagram shows the distances of some cities from London in kilometres.

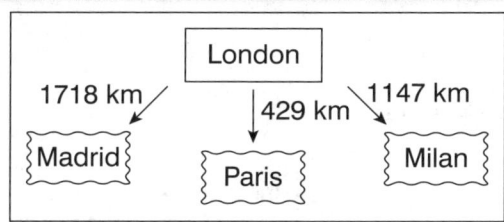

**6.** How much further is it from London to Madrid than from London to Paris?

_____

**7.** How much further is it from London to Madrid than from London to Milan?

_____

**8.** Answer these.

a)      3 0 2 9
      − 1 3 6 2
      _____

b)      5 6 1 4
      − 2 7 9 5
      _____

c)      7 2 0 4
      − 4 9 1 6
      _____

**9.** Write the difference between each pair.

a)   | 3.48 litres | 9.06 litres |   _____

b)   | 7.16 litres | 2.79 litres |   _____

**10.** A plank of wood is 2.14 metres in length. It is cut into two pieces. If one of the pieces is 0.79 metres, what is the length of the other piece?

_____

| 0.79 m |                    |
|←                      2.14 m                      →|

/10

1. Double each of these numbers.

a)  316 → [ ]     b)  185 → [ ]     c)  259 → [ ]

2. This is a ×80 machine. Complete the table.

| IN | 6 | | 3 | | 9 |
|---|---|---|---|---|---|
| OUT | | 560 | | 400 | |

3. Answer these. Show your method in the boxes below.

a) 59 × 6 = [ ]                    b) 74 × 8 = [ ]

4. Tick the multiplication that has the largest product.

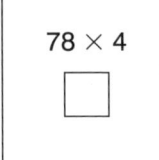 78 × 4  [ ]     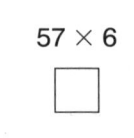 57 × 6  [ ]     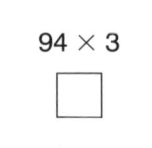 94 × 3  [ ]     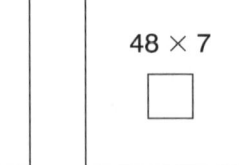 48 × 7  [ ]

5. A magazine costs £3.48 per month. What is the cost for 6 months subscription to the magazine?

_____

£3.48

**6.** Answer these. Show your method in the boxes below.

**a)** 38 × 49 = ⬜

**b)** 57 × 26 = ⬜

**7.** What is the area of each of these rectangles?

**a)**

17 cm

12 cm

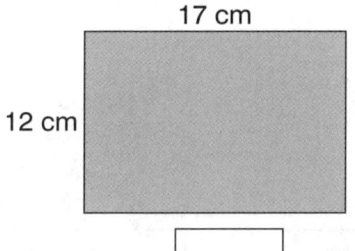

Area = ⬜ cm²

**b)**

23 cm

19 cm

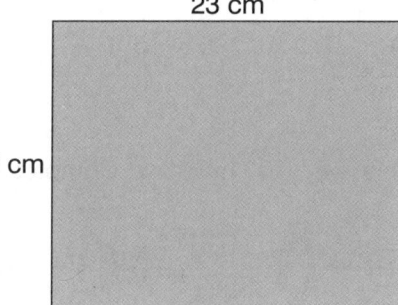

Area = ⬜ cm²

**8.** A box weighs 28 kg. What is the weight of 15 boxes? _____

**9.** Answer these.

**a)**
```
   3 7 4
 ×     8
 _____

 _____
```

**b)**
```
   2 0 9
 ×     6
 _____

 _____
```

**c)**
```
   4 7 8
 ×     4
 _____

 _____
```

**10.** What is the product of 425 and 9? _____

/10

1. Answer these. Show your method in the boxes below.

   **a)**  67 ÷ 4 =

   **b)**  106 ÷ 3 =

2. Write the missing numbers in each of these.

   **a)**  _____ ÷ 8 = 15

   **b)**  _____ ÷ 3 = 19

3. This is a ÷100 machine. Complete the table.

| IN | 490 | | 245 | | 705 |
|---|---|---|---|---|---|
| OUT | | 3.7 | | 6.81 | |

4. Answer these.

   **a)**  6 ) 8 4

   **b)**  5 ) 9 5

   **c)**  7 ) 9 1

5. Tick the numbers that are not exactly divisible by 3.

   | 143 | 219 | 171 | 206 | 316 | 378 |
   |---|---|---|---|---|---|
   | ☐ | ☐ | ☐ | ☐ | ☐ | ☐ |

**6.** Answer these.

**a)** 4 ) 3 7 5

**b)** 5 ) 8 3 6

**c)** 3 ) 5 0 9

**7.** A tube holds 6 tennis balls. How many tubes are needed for each of these quantities? Some of the tubes may not be full.

**a)** 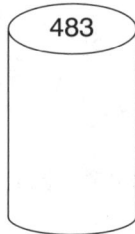 483

**b)** 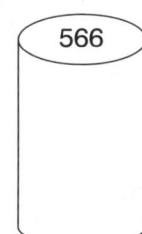 566

**c)** 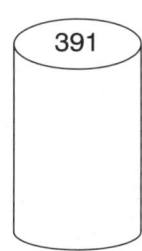 391

**d)** 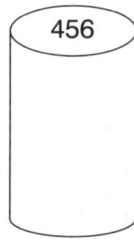 456

**8.** Write the missing digits to complete these.

**a)**  ☐ 4 9 r ☐
   5 ) 7 4 9

**b)**     3 5 r ☐
   8 ) ☐ 8 5

**c)**     5 ☐ 9 r ☐
   9 ) 5 ☐ 7

**9.** Which number between 90 and 100 has a remainder of 1 when it is divided by 8?

_____

**10.** What is the smallest number you can add to 490 to make it exactly divisible by 4?

_____

/10

**1.** Answer each of these.

a)
| $\frac{3}{5}$ of |
|---|
| 25 → _____ |
| 40 → _____ |
| 50 → _____ |
| 65 → _____ |

b)
| $\frac{2}{3}$ of |
|---|
| 24 → _____ |
| 30 → _____ |
| 42 → _____ |
| 90 → _____ |

**2.** Answer these.

a) 10% of £2 = _____
b) 25% of £20 = _____
c) 20% of £10 = _____

**3.** In a maths test, Emma scored 18 out of 20. The following week she scored 45 out of 50 in a different test. What were the percentage scores for each test?

a) $\frac{18}{20}$ = _____ %

b) $\frac{45}{50}$ = _____ %

**4.** What fraction of the grid is left white? Write it in its simplest form.

_____

**5.** What is $\frac{3}{4}$ of each of these?

a) | 52 kg |

_____ kg

b) | 600 ml |

_____ ml

c) | 900 g |

_____ g

d) | 120 cm |

_____ cm

# Answer booklet: Maths 10 Minute Tests age 9–10

**Test 1**
1. 107  118  129
2. 8  −16  −22
3. −2  −11
4. −4°C
5. 2°C
6. −8  1  7
7. −13  −4
8. −2°C
9. −7°C
10. 10  −6  −14

**Test 2**
1. 6.45 ➔ $6\frac{45}{100}$
   6.5 ➔ $6\frac{5}{10}$
   4.65 ➔ $4\frac{65}{100}$
   5.6 ➔ $5\frac{6}{10}$
   6.54 ➔ $6\frac{54}{100}$
2. 6.1  6.5  7.2  7.8
3. a) 0.34  b) 0.19  c) 0.07
4. a) $\frac{51}{100}$  b) $\frac{92}{100}$  c) $\frac{8}{100}$
5. a) 3.84  b) 5.12  c) 4.29
6. 3.51  3.57  3.63  3.66
7. a) 9 tenths
   b) 8 hundredths
   c) 0 tenths
8. 0.01  0.21  0.9
9. 486.79
10. a) $6\frac{24}{100}$  b) $3\frac{21}{100}$  c) $7\frac{55}{100}$

**Test 3**
1. a) 20 056 < 20 506
   b) 39 989 > 39 898
2. a) 745.5  b) 36.85  c) 1270.03
3. 20 868  20 886  20 905
   29 906  29 945
4. 30.19 kg
5. a) 0.01 < 0.11  b) 0.40 = 0.4
   c) 0.65 > 0.56
6. −7°C  −1°C
7. 37.45 m  37.5 m  37.91 m
   38.3 m  38.33 m
8. £74.88  £60.90  £40.05
   £38.70  £31.29
9. a) 7500  b) 25 000
10. −20°C  −19°C  −17°C
    −11°C  0°C  3°C

**Test 4**
1. 6535 ➔ 6540
   6575 ➔ 6580
   6548 ➔ 6550
   6556 ➔ 6560
   6573 ➔ 6570
2. a) 6869 ➔ 6900
   b) 8055 ➔ 8100
   c) 9344 ➔ 9300
3. a) £18.48 ➔ £18
   b) £27.52 ➔ £28
   c) £49.61 ➔ £50
4. Any two numbers between
   11.5 and 12.49
5. a) 100 g  b) 200 g  c) 400 g
6. Approximately 1800 ml
7. a) 400  b) 200
8. a) 438 + 327 ➔ 770
   b) 902 − 578 ➔ 320
9. 52.83 ➔ 53
   52.08 ➔ 52
   55.19 ➔ 55
   53.51 ➔ 54
10. 600–700 hours (696 hours)

**Test 5**
1. a) $\frac{11}{4}$  b) $\frac{4}{3}$
2. a) $\frac{9}{2} = 4\frac{1}{2}$  b) $\frac{15}{4} = 3\frac{3}{4}$
   c) $\frac{18}{5} = 3\frac{3}{5}$  d) $\frac{20}{3} = 6\frac{2}{3}$
3.

| Fractions | Decimals | Percentages |
|-----------|----------|-------------|
| $\frac{1}{2}$ | 0.5 | 50% |
| $\frac{1}{5}$ | 0.2 | 20% |
| $\frac{3}{4}$ | 0.75 | 75% |
| $\frac{3}{10}$ | 0.3 | 30% |

4. 65%
5. a) $\frac{35}{100} = 35\%$  b) $\frac{1}{4} = 25\%$
   c) $\frac{40}{50} = 80\%$
6.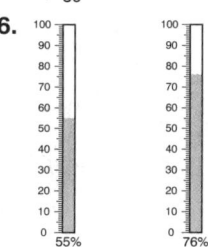

**Test 6**
1. a) $\frac{4}{10} = \frac{2}{5}$  b) $\frac{3}{5} = \frac{6}{10}$
2. a) $\frac{14}{16}$  b) $\frac{12}{25}$
3. $\frac{2}{5} = \frac{4}{10} = \frac{6}{15} = \frac{8}{20} = \frac{10}{25}$
4. $\frac{5}{8}$
5. a) $\frac{3}{10} = \frac{15}{50}$  b) $\frac{5}{6} = \frac{15}{18}$
   c) $\frac{2}{3} = \frac{40}{60}$
6.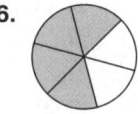
7. $\frac{6}{8} = \frac{3}{4}$
8. $\frac{5}{8} = \frac{10}{16} = \frac{15}{24} = \frac{20}{32} = \frac{25}{40}$
9. a) $\frac{6}{15} = \frac{2}{5}$  b) $\frac{25}{100} = \frac{1}{4}$
   c) $\frac{14}{16} = \frac{7}{8}$
10. Check that the fractions that
    are equivalent to $\frac{3}{5}$

**Test 7**
1. 3 red and 9 blue tiles
2. 3 green and 12 yellow tiles
3. 6 black and 10 white tiles
4. 200 g of cherries
5. $\frac{1}{3}$
6. $\frac{3}{5}$
7. 200 g fish
   500 g potatoes
   100 g peas
   80 g cheese
   40 g butter
   60 ml milk
8. 1 to 2 or 1:2
9. 16 pages
10. 3 to 4 or 3:4

7. $\frac{1}{5}$ ➔ 0.2 ➔ 20%
   $\frac{3}{10}$ ➔ 0.3 ➔ 30%
   $\frac{45}{100}$ ➔ 0.45 ➔ 45%
   $\frac{4}{5}$ ➔ 0.8 ➔ 80%
8. a) 90% = $\frac{90}{100}$ or $\frac{9}{10}$
   b) 5% = $\frac{5}{100}$ or $\frac{1}{20}$
   c) 60% = $\frac{60}{100}$ or $\frac{3}{5}$ or $\frac{6}{10}$
9. a) 0.8 > 8%  b) 0.2 < 50%
   c) 0.25 < 75%
10. a) $4\frac{3}{4}$ ➔ $\frac{19}{4}$  b) $2\frac{1}{2}$ ➔ $\frac{5}{2}$
    c) $5\frac{2}{3}$ ➔ $\frac{17}{3}$

## Test 8

1. a) $7 \times 8 = 56$    b) $6 \times 9 = 54$
   c) $4 \times 8 = 32$

2. a)

| × | 7 | 9 | 6 |
|---|---|---|---|
| 8 | 56 | 72 | 48 |
| 7 | 49 | 63 | 42 |
| 4 | 28 | 36 | 24 |

b)

| × | 10 | 11 | 12 |
|---|----|----|----|
| 8 | 80 | 88 | 96 |
| 9 | 90 | 99 | 108 |
| 10 | 100 | 110 | 120 |

3. a) $27 \div 3 = 9$    b) $42 \div 6 = 7$
   c) $56 \div 7 = 8$

4. 24 and 48

5. $25 \div 3 \rightarrow$ r1
   $44 \div 5 \rightarrow$ r4
   $68 \div 9 \rightarrow$ r5
   $51 \div 8 \rightarrow$ r3
   $44 \div 6 \rightarrow$ r2

6. $36 \rightarrow$ Any 2 from $2 \times 18$, $3 \times 12$,
   $4 \times 9$
   $60 \rightarrow$ Any 2 from $2 \times 30$, $3 \times 20$,
   $4 \times 15$, $5 \times 12$, $6 \times 10$
   $40 \rightarrow$ Any 2 from $2 \times 20$, $4 \times 10$,
   $5 \times 8$
   $72 \rightarrow$ Any 2 from $2 \times 36$, $3 \times 24$,
   $4 \times 18$, $6 \times 12$, $8 \times 9$

7. a)

| × | 9 | 5 | 6 |
|---|---|---|---|
| 3 | 27 | 15 | 18 |
| 8 | 72 | 40 | 48 |
| 7 | 63 | 35 | 42 |

b)

| × | 7 | 4 | 8 |
|---|---|---|---|
| 8 | 56 | 32 | 64 |
| 9 | 63 | 36 | 72 |
| 3 | 21 | 12 | 24 |

8. a) $30 \times 6 = 180$
   b) $50 \times 4 = 200$
   c) $50 \times 7 = 350$

9. 30

10. 4

## Test 9

1. a) $32 \rightarrow$ 1, 2, 4, 8, 16, 32
   b) $20 \rightarrow$ 1, 2, 4, 5, 10, 20
   c) $25 \rightarrow$ 1, 5, 25
   d) $55 \rightarrow$ 1, 5, 11, 55

2. a) The 5th multiple of 4 is 20
   b) The 6th multiple of 3 is 18
   c) The 4th multiple of 9 is 36

3. The three smallest multiples
   are:
   a) 12, 24, 36    b) 15, 30, 45

4. a) $28 \rightarrow$ (1,28) (2,14) (4,7)
   b) $45 \rightarrow$ (1,45) (3,15) (5,9)
   c) $40 \rightarrow$ (1,40) (2,20) (4,10) (5,8)
   d) $24 \rightarrow$ (1,24) (2,12) (3,8) (4,6)

5. True

6. 30, 45, 60

7. 45, 27

8. 60

9. a) A common multiple of 5 and
   7 is 70
   b) A common multiple of 3 and
   8 is 48

10. False

## Test 10

1. a) 161    b) 216    c) 218

2. a) 1175 and 3825
   b) 3281 and 1719
   c) 2386 and 2614
   d) 2208 and 2792

3. a) 311   b) 367   c) 423   d) 641

4. 20.2 cm

5.

| 7.2 | 9.1 | 16.3 |
|-----|-----|------|
| 6.4 | 8.9 | 15.3 |
| 13.6 | 18 | 31.6 |

6. a) 6744    b) 9190    c) 8651

7. £56.44

8. 8 and 6    1 and 2    2 and 9

9. £18.75 $\rightarrow$ £11.25
   £19.75 $\rightarrow$ £10.25
   £12.55 $\rightarrow$ £17.45
   £15.85 $\rightarrow$ £14.15

10. $349 + 76 = 425$

## Test 11

1. 154 $\rightarrow$ 66
   127 $\rightarrow$ 39
   134 $\rightarrow$ 46
   119 $\rightarrow$ 31

2. a) 125    b) 246    c) 358

3. a) £6.42   b) £1.73   c) £3.91

4. a) 4, 2    b) 7, 2    c) 7, 2, 9

5. 344

6. 1289 km

7. 571 km

8. a) 1667   b) 2819   c) 2288

9. a) 5.58 litres    b) 4.37 litres

10. 1.35 metres

## Test 12

1. a) 316 $\rightarrow$ 632    b) 185 $\rightarrow$ 370
   c) 259 $\rightarrow$ 518

2.

| IN | 6 | 7 | 3 | 5 | 9 |
|----|---|---|---|---|---|
| OUT | 480 | 560 | 240 | 400 | 720 |

3. a) 354    b) 592

4. $57 \times 6 = 342$

5. £20.88

6. a) 1862    b) 1482

7. a) 204 cm²    b) 437 cm²

8. 420 kg

9. a) 2992    b) 1254    c) 1912

10. 3825

## Test 13

1. a) $67 \div 4 = 16$ r 3
   b) $106 \div 3 = 35$ r 1

2. a) $120 \div 8 = 15$
   b) $57 \div 3 = 19$

3.

| IN | 490 | 370 | 245 | 681 | 705 |
|----|-----|-----|-----|-----|-----|
| OUT | 4.9 | 3.7 | 2.45 | 6.81 | 7.05 |

4. a) 14    b) 19    c) 13

5. 143        206        316

6. a) 93 r 3   b) 167 r 1   c) 169 r 2

7. a) 483 $\rightarrow$ 81
   b) 566 $\rightarrow$ 95
   c) 391 $\rightarrow$ 66
   d) 456 $\rightarrow$ 76

8. a) $\begin{array}{r} 149 \text{ r } 4 \\ 5 \overline{)749} \end{array}$    b) $\begin{array}{r} 35 \text{ r } 5 \\ 8 \overline{)285} \end{array}$

   c) $\begin{array}{r} 59 \text{ r } 6 \\ 9 \overline{)537} \end{array}$

9. 97

10. 2

## Test 14

1. a) $\frac{3}{5}$ of…        b) $\frac{2}{3}$ of…

   25 $\rightarrow$ 15        24 $\rightarrow$ 16
   40 $\rightarrow$ 24        30 $\rightarrow$ 20
   50 $\rightarrow$ 30        42 $\rightarrow$ 28
   65 $\rightarrow$ 39        90 $\rightarrow$ 60

2. a) 20p    b) £5    c) £2

3. a) $\frac{18}{20} = 90\%$    b) $\frac{45}{50} = 90\%$

4. $\frac{4}{9}$

5. a) 39 kg        b) 450 ml
   c) 675 g        d) 90 cm

6. flour 240 g
   butter 160 g
   sugar 80 g
   raisins 200 g
   cherries 80 g
   walnuts 40 g

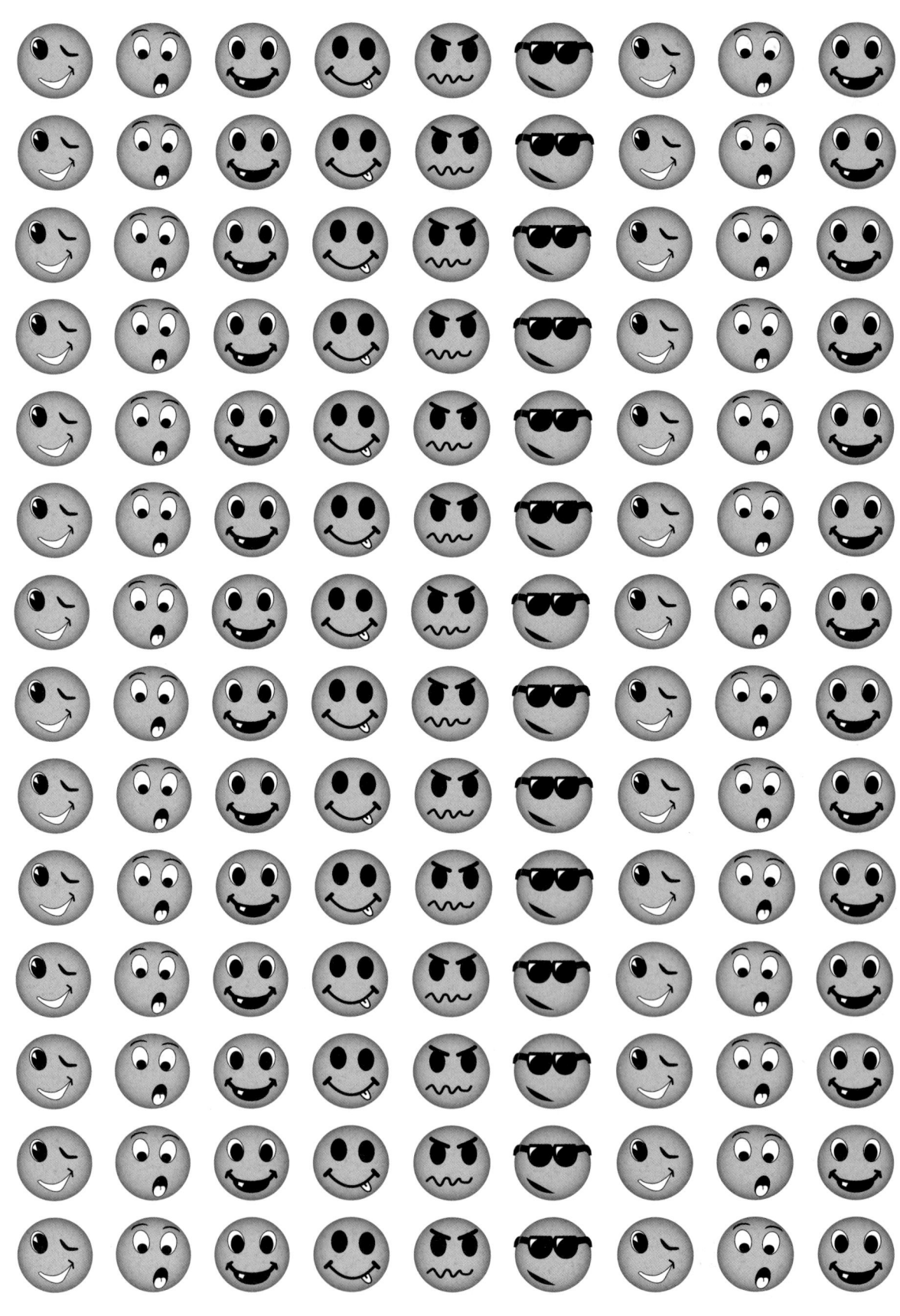

**7.** a) 10% of £75 = £7.50
b) 20% of £75 = £15
c) 5% of £75 = £3.75
d) 15% of £75 = £11.25

**8.** $\frac{1}{6}$

**9.** $\frac{4}{7}$ of 63 litres

**10.** a) 80 kg → 4 kg
b) 30 kg → 1.5 kg
c) 140 kg → 7 kg

## Test 15

**1.**
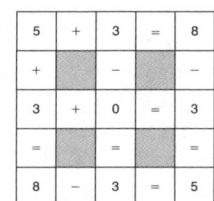

| 5 | + | 3 | = | 8 |
|---|---|---|---|---|
| + | | – | | – |
| 3 | + | 0 | = | 3 |
| = | | = | | = |
| 8 | – | 3 | = | 5 |

**2.**

| 4 | + | 4 | = | 8 |
|---|---|---|---|---|
| + | | × | | – |
| 5 | + | 2 | = | 7 |
| = | | = | | = |
| 9 | – | 8 | = | 1 |

**3.**

| 4 | + | 6 | = | 10 |
|---|---|---|---|---|
| × | | ÷ | | – |
| 3 | × | 2 | = | 6 |
| = | | = | | = |
| 12 | ÷ | 3 | = | 4 |

**4.**

| 12 | ÷ | 6 | = | 2 |
|---|---|---|---|---|
| – | | ÷ | | × |
| 8 | – | 2 | = | 6 |
| = | | = | | = |
| 4 | × | 3 | = | 12 |

**5.**

| 24 | ÷ | 6 | = | 4 |
|---|---|---|---|---|
| ÷ | | × | | × |
| 12 | ÷ | 2 | = | 6 |
| = | | = | | = |
| 2 | × | 12 | = | 24 |

**6.**

| 6 | × | 6 | = | 36 |
|---|---|---|---|---|
| × | | ÷ | | ÷ |
| 1 | × | 6 | = | 6 |
| = | | = | | = |
| 6 | × | 1 | = | 6 |

## Test 16

**1.**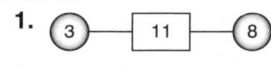

**2.**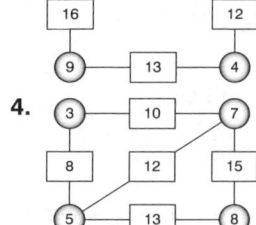

**3.**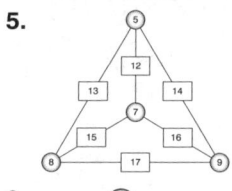

**4.**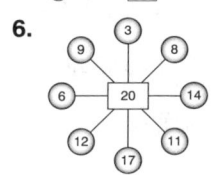

**5.** 

**6.**

## Test 17

**1.** pentagon   octagon

heptagon   hexagon

**2.**

| | A | B | C | D | E | F | G | H |
|---|---|---|---|---|---|---|---|---|
| equilateral | ✓ | | | | ✓ | | | ✓ |
| isosceles | | ✓ | ✓ | ✓ | | ✓ | ✓ | |

**3.** B and G
**4.** always true
**5.** rhombus or parallelogram
**6.**

Equilateral   Right angle

**7.** Check that a parallelogram or rhombus has been drawn.
**8.** sometimes true
**9.** 2nd, 4th and 5th shapes should be ticked.
**10.** Check line is perpendicular to AB.

## Test 18

**1.**

| | A | B | C | D | E | F | G |
|---|---|---|---|---|---|---|---|
| prisms | ✓ | ✓ | | | | ✓ | |
| pyramids | | | ✓ | ✓ | ✓ | | ✓ |

**2.** 6 faces, 12 edges and 8 vertices
**3.** a) triangular pyramid or tetrahedron
b) triangular prism
**4.** sometimes true
**5.** 6 vertices
**6.** The 5th shape should be ticked.
**7.** 6 edges
**8.** a) square-based pyramid
b) pentagonal prism
**9.** cylinder
**10.** Check accuracy of drawings.

## Test 19

**1–5.**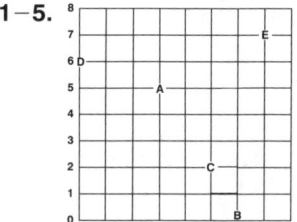

**6.** rectangle → (2,3)
**7.** pentagon → (5,8)
**8.** square → (1,7)
**9.** triangle → (7,5)
**10.** circle → (4,1)

## Test 20

**1.** West
**2.** North-East
**3.** North
**4.** South-West
**5.** South-East
**6–10.**

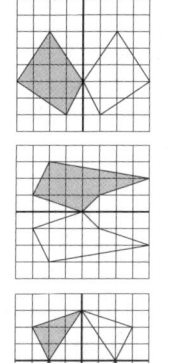
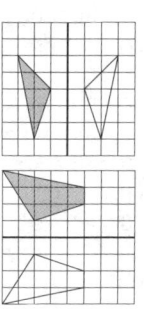

**Test 21**

1.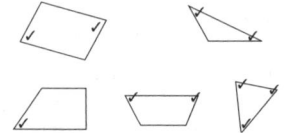

2. Check that an obtuse angle has been drawn.
3. a) 40°     b) 110°
4. 360°
5. True
6. 65°
7. 180°
8. 270°
9. a) 60°     b) 135°     c) 80°
10. a) 60°     b) 20°     c) 55°

**Test 22**

1. a) 4.2 m = 420 cm
   b) 6.3 km = 6300 m
   c) 78 mm = 7.8 cm
   d) 80 cm = 0.8 m
2. 3.8 m
3. 850 g
4. 2.2 l
5. 8 cm = 80 mm
6. 5.15 km or 5150 m
7. a) 6.7 kg = 6700 g
   b) 3.95 kg = 3950 g
   c) 8200 g = 8.2 kg
   d) 4750 g = 4.75 kg
8. 15 mm
9. a) 1450 g + 3550 g
   b) 2850 g + 2150 g
10. a) 5.9 l = 5900 ml
    b) 8.65 l = 8650 ml
    c) 3400 ml = 3.4 l
    d) 7250 ml = 7.25 l

**Test 23**

1. a) 1.6 kg     b) 24 kg
2. a) 55 mm     b) 120 mm
3. a) 1400 ml     b) 1900 ml
4. 25 mm     85 mm
5. 60 mm
6. 300 ml
7. a) 1.8 kg     b) 15 kg
8. 13.2 kg
9. a) 3.3 l     b) 2.25 l
10. 2.2 kg

**Test 24**

1. Check rectangle has a perimeter of 30 squares.
2. 140 mm

3. 9.4 m
4. 9 m
5. 226 mm
6. Check both shapes have a perimeter of 14 cm.
7. 36 cm
8. 11 mm
9. 37.8 m
10. 249 mm

**Test 25**

1. 153 cm²
2. Check that the area of each shape is 14 squares².
3. 144 cm²
4. 6 cm
5. 750 cm²
6. Check that the area of each shape is 24 cm²
7. 28 cm
8. a) Area of A = 36 cm²
   b) Area of B = 12 cm²
9. Total area = 48 cm²
10. 8 cm

**Test 26**

1. a) 8 o'clock in the morning ➔ 08:00
   b) 8 o'clock in the evening ➔ 20:00
2. 16:20
3. a) 08:55     b) 11:05     c) 14:25
4. a) 1800 seconds = 30 minutes
   b) $10\frac{1}{2}$ minutes = 630 seconds
   c) $8\frac{1}{2}$ hours = 510 minutes
   d) 720 hours = 30 days
5. 3.08 p.m.
6. a)      b)      c)
7. Wednesday 30ᵗʰ April
8. a) 16:45 ➔ 4.45 p.m.
   b) 11:53 ➔ 11.53 a.m.
   c) 23:05 ➔ 11.05 p.m.
9.

| Aston | 10:42 | 14:10 | 18.14 |
| Bunstone | 11:57 | 15:25 | 19:29 |
| Caleby | 13:12 | 16:40 | 20:44 |

10. a) 10.35 p.m. ➔ 22:35
    b) 8.49 a.m. ➔ 08:49
    c) 3.55 p.m. ➔ 15:55

**Test 27**

1. Check answer – if snow on ground could be good chance, if not then poor chance
2. even chance
3. Check answer – good chance is likely, but chips may not be liked!
4. certain
5. even chance
6. a 6 – poor chance
   a number greater than 8 – impossible
   an odd number – even chance
   a number less than 7 – certain
7. even chance
8. poor chance
9. good chance
10. impossible

**Test 28**

1. 17 children
2. 5 children
3. 51 children
4. 29 children
5. Scores between 31 and 35 correct answers
6. 10.00 a.m.
7. 27 km
8. 11.20 a.m.
9. 40 km
10. 1 hour 40 minutes

**Test 29**

Check that the shapes have one extra triangle drawn to make each of them symmetrical.

**Test 30**

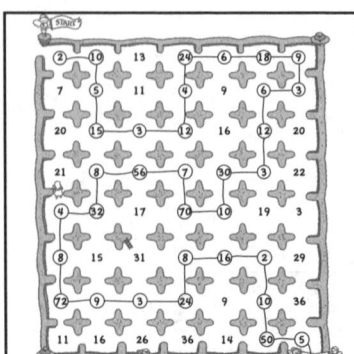

Alternative answers are possible.

## Fractions and percentages

**6.** These are the ingredients for an 800 g cake. Write the weight of each ingredient.

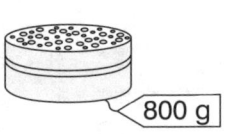

800 g

**Recipe**

30% flour
20% butter
10% sugar
25% raisins
10% cherries
5% walnuts

**Ingredients**

flour _____ g
butter _____ g
sugar _____ g
raisins _____ g
cherries _____ g
walnuts _____ g

**7.** Answer these.

**a)**

10% of £75 = ____

**b)**

20% of £75 = ____

**c)**

5% of £75 = ____

**d)**

15% of £75 = ____

**8.** A bag contains 60 marbles. $\frac{1}{3}$ of them are red, $\frac{2}{5}$ of them are blue and $\frac{1}{10}$ of them are yellow. The rest of the marbles are green. What fraction of the marbles in the bag are green?

_____

**9.** Circle the largest amount.

$\frac{5}{8}$ of 56 litres          $\frac{4}{7}$ of 63 litres

**10.** What is 5% of each of these?

**a)** 80 kg → _____     **b)** 30 kg → _____     **c)** 140 kg → _____

/10

## Number puzzles

Write the missing numbers on each of these grids.

**1.**

| 5 | + | 3 | = |   |
|---|---|---|---|---|
| + |   | − |   | − |
|   | + |   | = |   |
| = |   | = |   | = |
|   | − | 3 | = | 5 |

**2.**

| 4 | + | 4 | = |   |
|---|---|---|---|---|
| + |   | × |   | − |
|   | + |   | = | 7 |
| = |   | = |   | = |
| 9 | − |   | = |   |

**3.**

|   | + | 6 | = |   |
|---|---|---|---|---|
| × |   | ÷ |   | − |
| 3 | × |   | = |   |
| = |   | = |   | = |
| 12 | ÷ |   | = | 4 |

**4.**

|   | ÷ |   | = | 2 |
|---|---|---|---|---|
| − |   | ÷ |   | × |
|   | − | 2 | = |   |
| = |   | = |   | = |
| 4 | × |   | = | 12 |

**5.**

| 24 | ÷ | 6 | = |   |
|----|---|---|---|---|
| ÷ |   | × |   | × |
|   | ÷ | 2 | = |   |
| = |   | = |   | = |
|   | × |   | = | 24 |

**6.**

| 6 | × |   | = | 36 |
|---|---|---|---|----|
| × |   | ÷ |   | ÷ |
|   | × |   | = | 6 |
| = |   | = |   | = |
|   | × |   | = | 6 |

## Arithmogons

In each of these, the number in the square is the total of the two numbers in the circles on either side. Write the missing numbers.

1. ( 3 )—[ ]—( 8 )

2. 
( 5 )
[ ]   [ 13 ]
( 6 )—[ ]—( )

3. 
( )—[ ]—( 8 )
[ 16 ]        [ ]
( 9 )—[ 13 ]—( )

4. 
( )—[ 10 ]—( 7 )
[ 8 ]   [ ]   [ ]
( )—[ 13 ]—( )

5. 
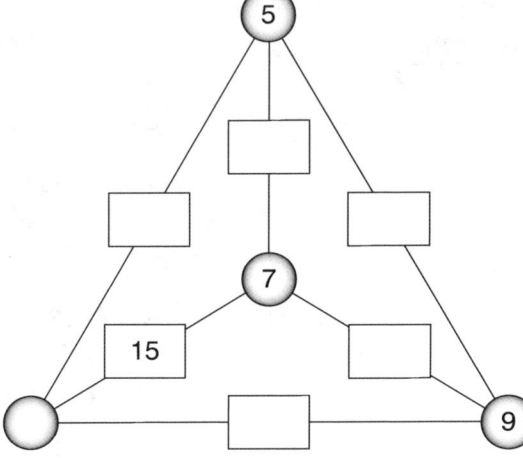

6. 
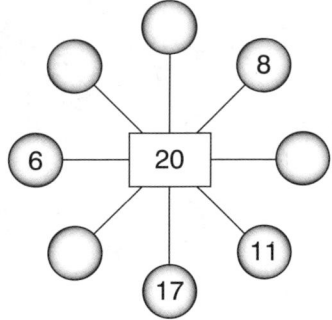

## 2-D shapes

**1.** Draw lines to match each name to the correct regular shape.

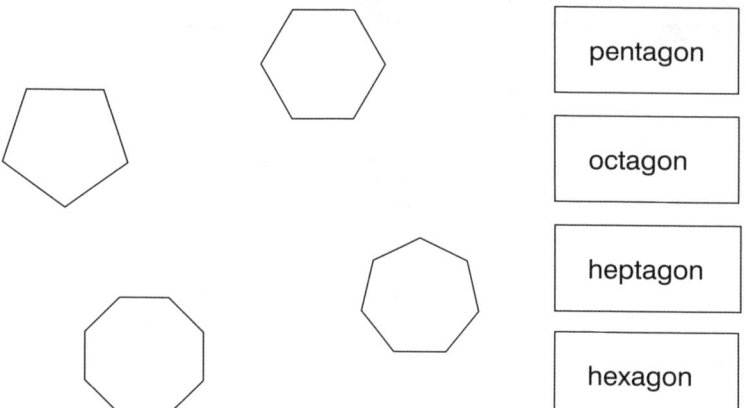

| pentagon |
| --- |

| octagon |

| heptagon |

| hexagon |

**2.** Complete the table for these triangles.

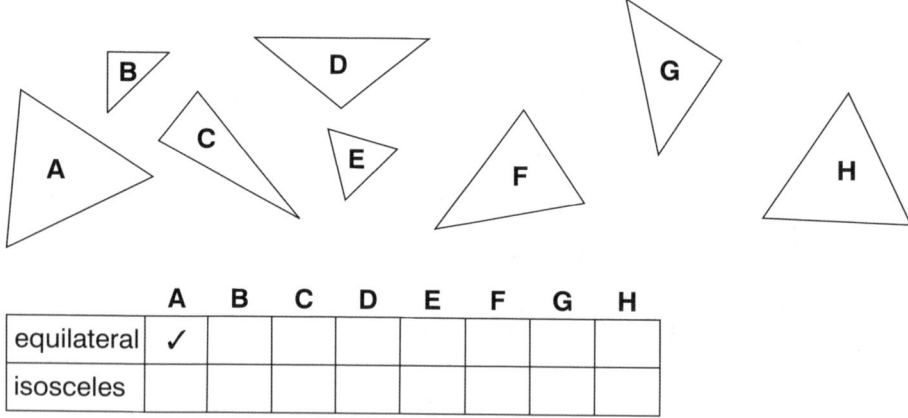

|  | A | B | C | D | E | F | G | H |
| --- | --- | --- | --- | --- | --- | --- | --- | --- |
| equilateral | ✓ |  |  |  |  |  |  |  |
| isosceles |  |  |  |  |  |  |  |  |

**3.** Which triangles have a right angle? _____

**4.** An isosceles triangle has a line of symmetry. Is this always, sometimes or never true?

_____

**5.** What is the name of this shape?

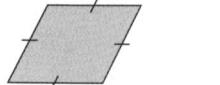 _____

**6.** Draw lines to join each triangle to the correct place on the Venn diagram.

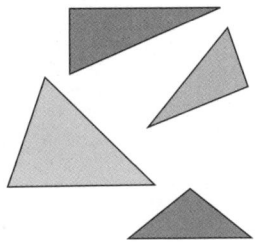
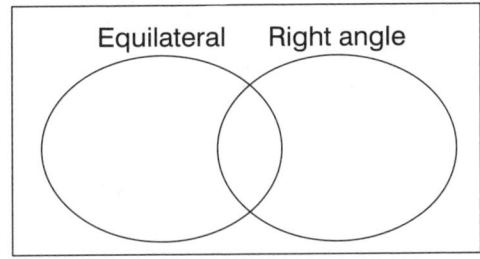

**7.** Draw a quadrilateral on this grid which has opposite sides of equal sides but no right angles.

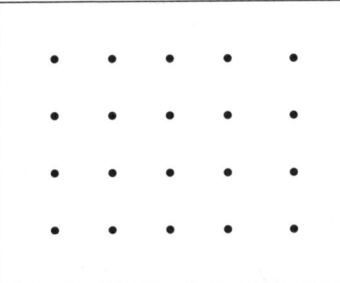

**8.** A quadrilateral is symmetrical. Is this always, sometimes or never true?

_____

**9.** Tick each shape that has parallel sides.

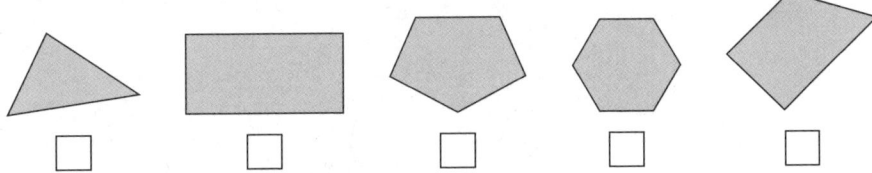

**10.** Draw a line perpendicular to AB from C.

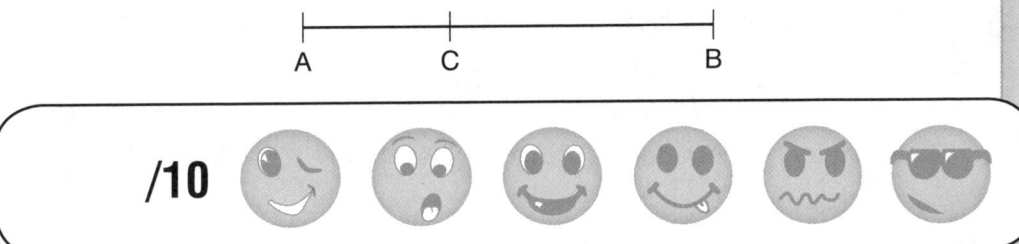

/10

**1.** Complete the table for these 3-D shapes.

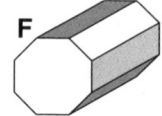
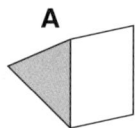
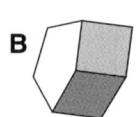

|          | A | B | C | D | E | F | G |
|----------|---|---|---|---|---|---|---|
| prisms   |   |   |   |   |   |   |   |
| pyramids |   |   |   |   |   |   |   |

**2.** How many faces, edges and vertices does a cube have?

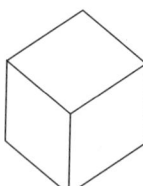

_____ faces

_____ edges

_____ vertices

**3.** Name the shapes made from each net.

a)

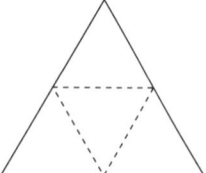

_____

b)

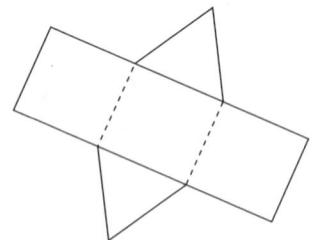

_____

**4.** A pyramid has four faces. Is this always, sometimes or never true?

_____

**5.** How many vertices does a triangular prism have?

_____

**6.** Tick the tetrahedron in this set of pyramids.

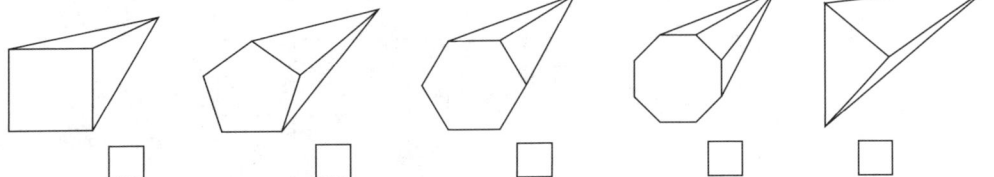

**7.** How many edges does a tetrahedron have? _____

**8.** Name the shapes made from each net.

a)

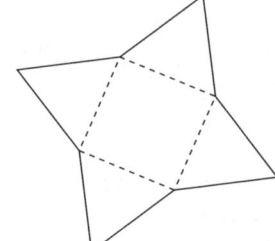

b)

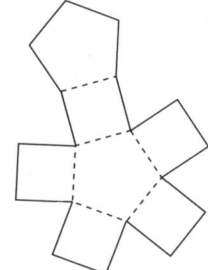

_____ _____

**9.** Name this 3-D shape.

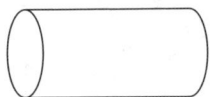

_____

**10.** Draw a prism and pyramid starting from a triangle.

a)

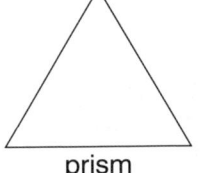

prism

b)

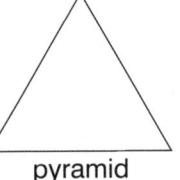

pyramid

**/10**

37

Write the letters in the correct positions on the grid for each of these.

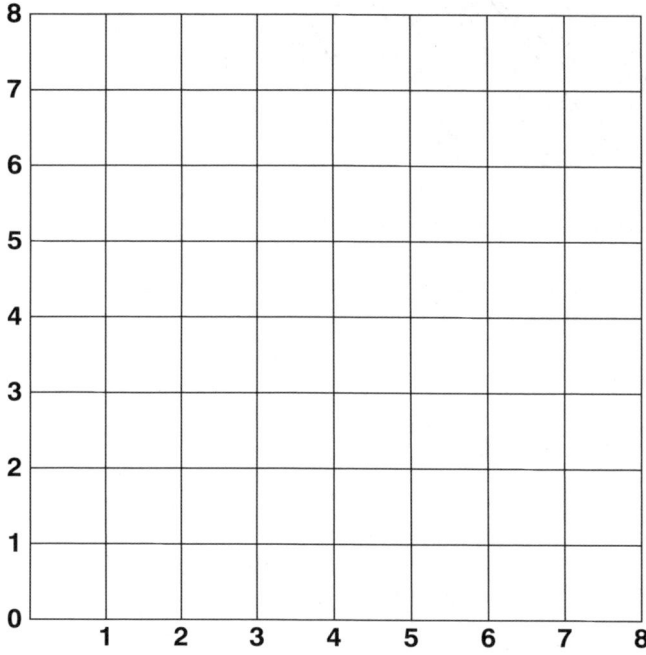

**1.** A → (3, 5)

**2.** B → (6, 0)

**3.** C → (5, 2)

**4.** D → (0, 6)

**5.** E → (7, 7)

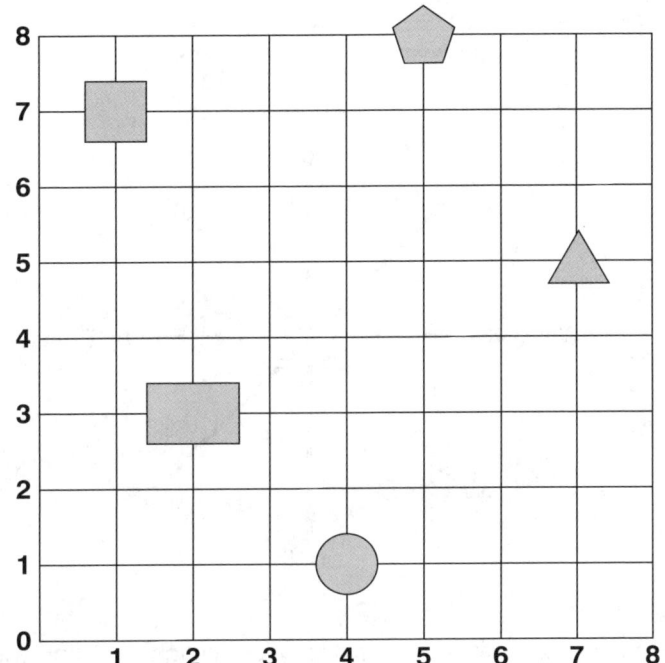

Write the position on the grid of each shape.

**6.** rectangle → _____

**7.** pentagon → _____

**8.** square → _____

**9.** triangle → _____

**10.** circle → _____

/10

## Movement geometry

Use the compass points to help you answer these.

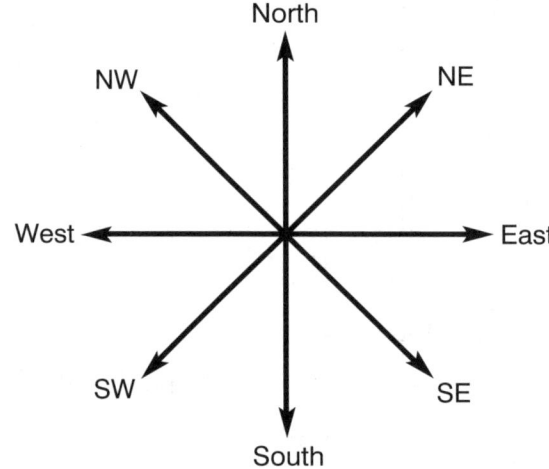

1. If I face north and make a quarter turn anticlockwise, which direction will I be facing?

   _____

2. If I face south-west and make a half turn clockwise, which direction will I be facing?

   _____

3. If I face east and make a 90° turn anticlockwise, which direction will I be facing?

   _____

4. If I face north-east and make a 180° turn clockwise, which direction will I be facing?

   _____

5. If I face south-east and make a 360° turn anticlockwise, which direction will I be facing?

   _____

Each of these grids has a mirror line. Draw the reflection of each shape on the grid.

**6.**

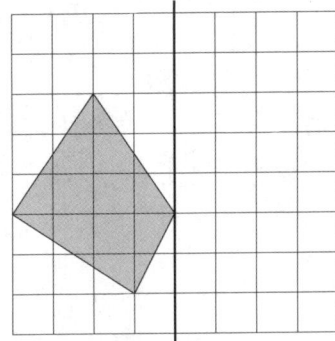

Mirror line

**7.**

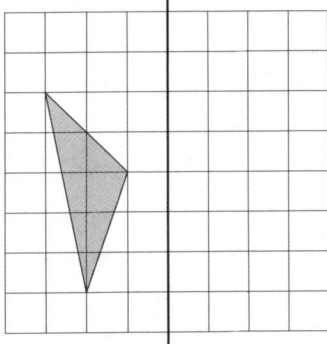

Mirror line

**8.**

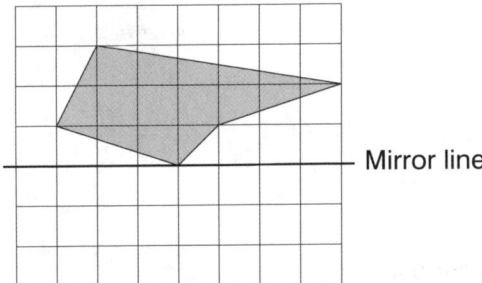

—— Mirror line

**9.**

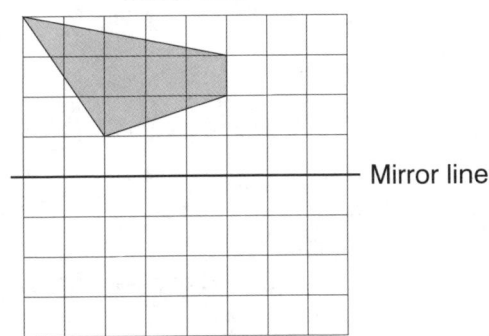

—— Mirror line

**10.** This grid has two mirror lines. Draw the reflection of the shape.

Mirror line

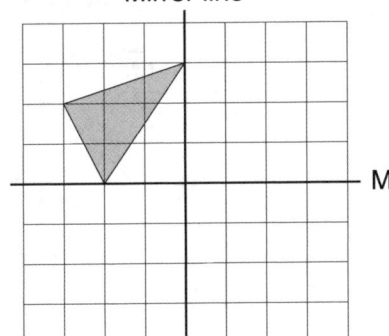

—— Mirror line

/10

**1.** Tick all the acute angles in these shapes.

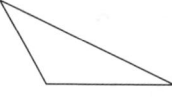

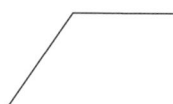

**2.** Draw an obtuse angle on this grid.

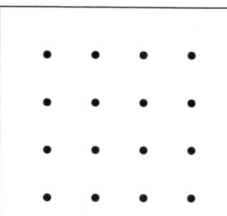

**3.** Estimate these angles. Circle the angles nearest your estimate.

**a)**

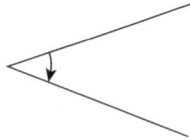

| 30° | 40° | 50° | 60° |

**b)**

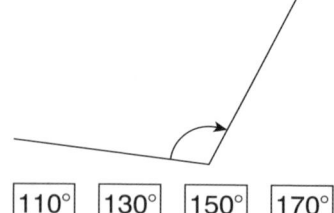

| 110° | 130° | 150° | 170° |

**4.** What is the angle sum of a rectangle?

_____

**5.** True or false? An obtuse angle is between 90° and 180°.

_____

6. Use a protractor or angle measurer to measure this angle.

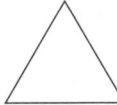

7. What is the angle sum of an equilateral triangle? _____

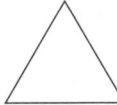

8. How many degrees are there in three right angles? _____

9. Write the size of the missing angles on these straight lines. Do not measure the angles.

a)

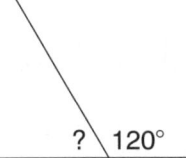

? \ 120°

b)

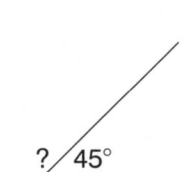

? / 45°

c)

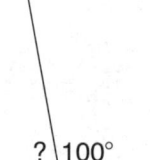

? \ 100°

10. Write the size of the missing angles on these right angles. Do not measure the angles.

a)

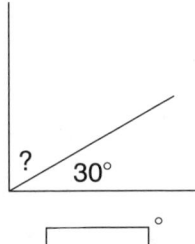

? 30°

b)

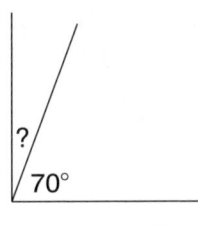

? 70°

c)

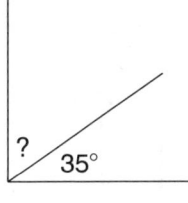

? 35°

/10

## Standard units of measure

**1.** Write these lengths.

   **a)**  4.2 m = _____ cm       **b)**  6.3 km = _____ m

   **c)**  78 mm = _____ cm     **d)**  80 cm = _____ m

> Underline the amount each item is most likely to measure.

**2.** My bedroom is (3.8 cm) (3.8 m) (30.8 m) (3.8 km) across from one wall to the other.

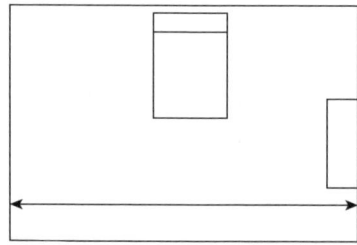

**3.** A loaf of bread weighs (85 g) (850 g) (8.5 kg) (8.5 g).

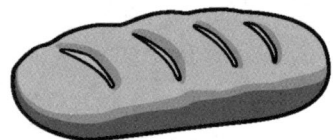

**4.** I put my (2.2 ml) (22 l) (22 ml) (2.2 l) carton of orange juice in the fridge.

**5.** Measure the length of this line in centimetres and millimetres.

      ☐ cm = ☐ mm

**6.** What is 850 m less than 6 km? _____ km or _____ m

**7.** Complete these.

   **a)** 6.7 kg = _____ g          **b)** 3.95 kg = _____ g

   **c)** 8200 g = _____ kg          **d)** 4750 g = _____ kg

**8.** What is the difference in length between these two lines? _____ mm

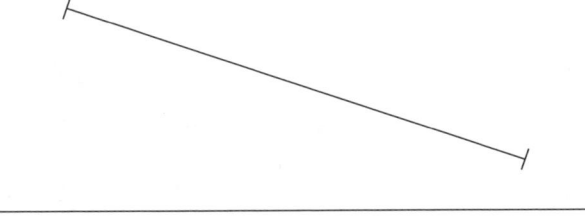

**9.** What must be added to each measurement to make 5 kg?

   **a)**

   1450 g + ☐ g

   **b)**

   2850 g + ☐ g

**10.** Complete these.

   **a)** 5.9 l = _____ ml          **b)** 8.65 l = _____ ml

   **c)** 3400 ml = _____ l          **d)** 7250 ml = _____ l

/10

## Reading scales

**1.** What is the reading on each of these scales?

**a)**

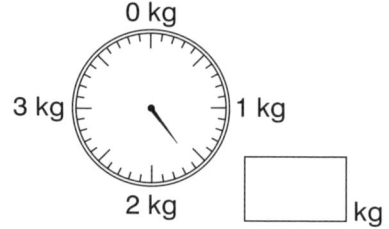

kg

**b)**

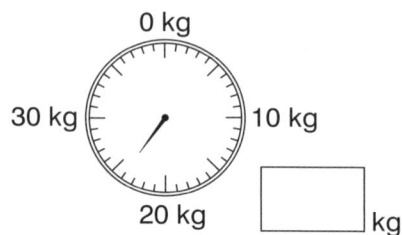

kg

**2.** Write each reading in millimetres.

**a)**

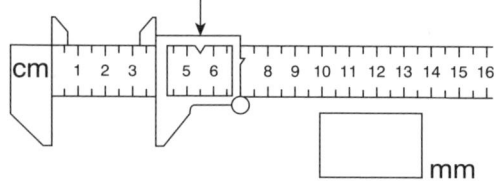

mm

**b)**

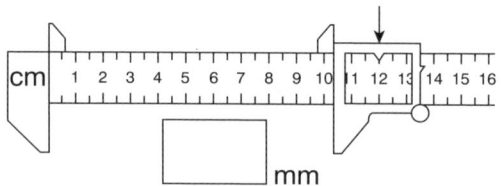

mm

**3.** How much liquid is in each jug? Write the amounts in millilitres.

**a)**

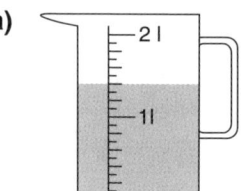

**b)**

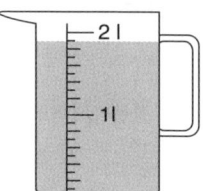

**4.** Write these lengths in millimetres.

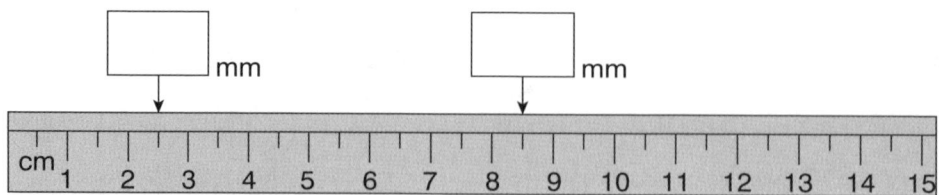

**5.** What is the distance between the arrows in Q 4?

Distance = [ ] mm

**6.** 110 ml of liquid is added to this container. How much liquid will there be in total?

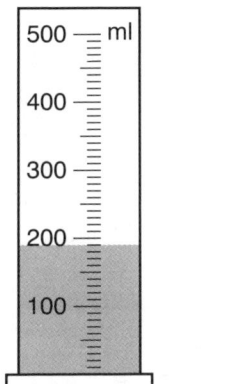

_____ ml

**7.** What is the reading on each of these scales?

**a)**

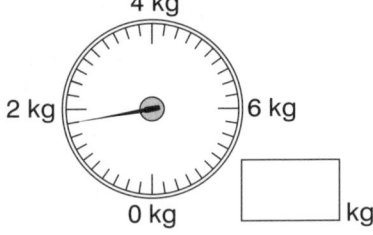

[        ] kg

**b)**

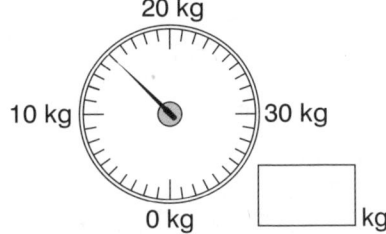

[        ] kg

**8.** What is the difference between the two amounts shown above? _____

**9.** How much liquid is in each jug? Write the amounts in litres.

**a)**

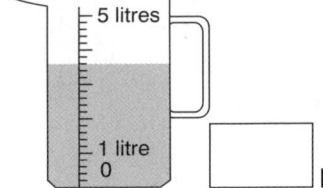

[        ] l

**b)**

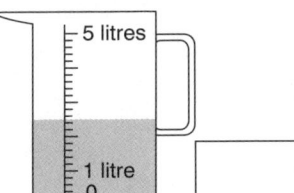

[        ] l

**10.** 400 g of flour is taken off these scales.
What will the new reading be?

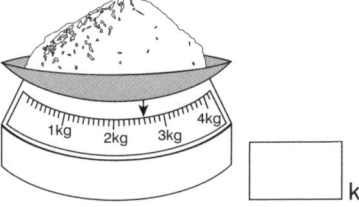

[        ] kg

/10

47

## Perimeter

**1.** Draw a rectangle on this grid with a perimeter of 30 squares.

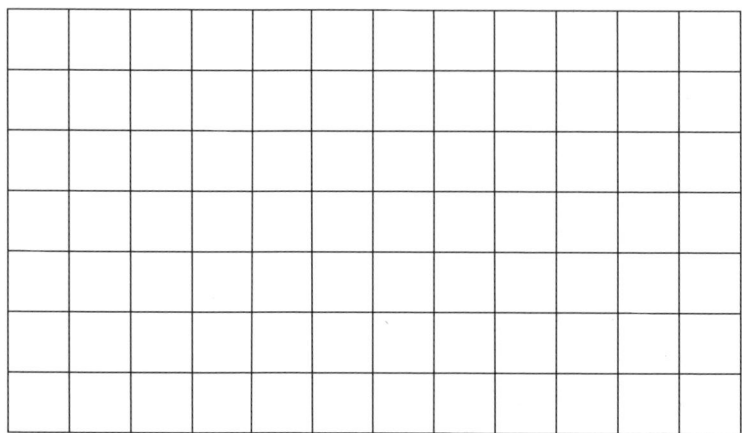

**2.** A square has sides of 35 mm each. What is the perimeter of the square?

_____mm

**3.** What is the perimeter of this rectangle?

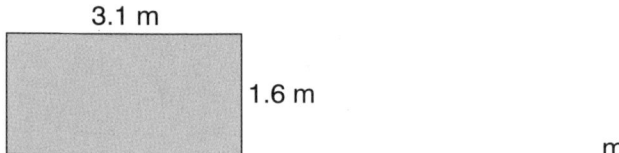

3.1 m

1.6 m

_____m

**4.** What is the perimeter of a regular pentagon with sides of 1.8 metres each?

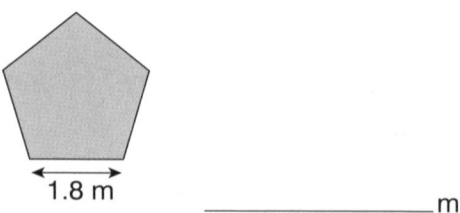

1.8 m          _____m

**5.** What is the perimeter of this shape?

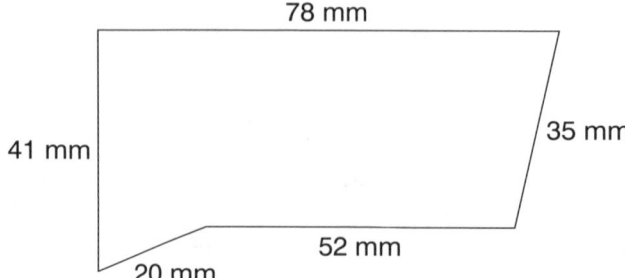

78 mm

41 mm

35 mm

52 mm

20 mm

_____mm

**6.** Draw two different shapes on this grid, each with a perimeter of 14 cm.

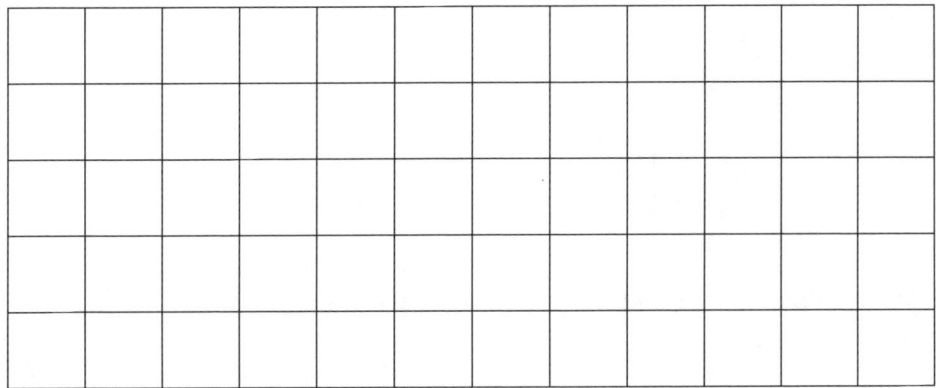

**7.** What is the perimeter of a square with an area of 81 cm²? _____ cm

**8.** A rectangle has a perimeter of 64 mm. If the length of each of the longest sides is 21 mm,

what is the length of each of the shortest sides? _____ mm

**9.** What is the perimeter of this shape?

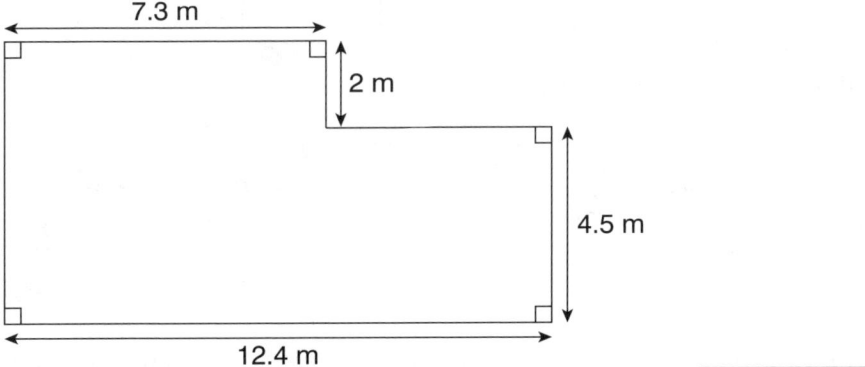

_____ m

**10.** What is the perimeter of an equilateral triangle with sides of 8.3 cm?

_____ mm

/10

1. What is the area of this rectangle?

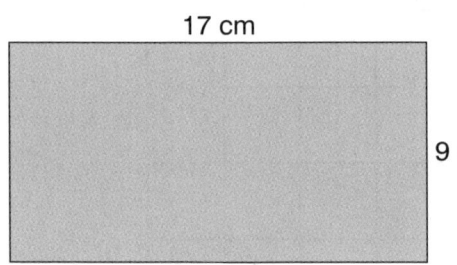

17 cm

9 cm

_____ cm²

2. Draw two different shapes on this grid, each with an area of 14 squares.

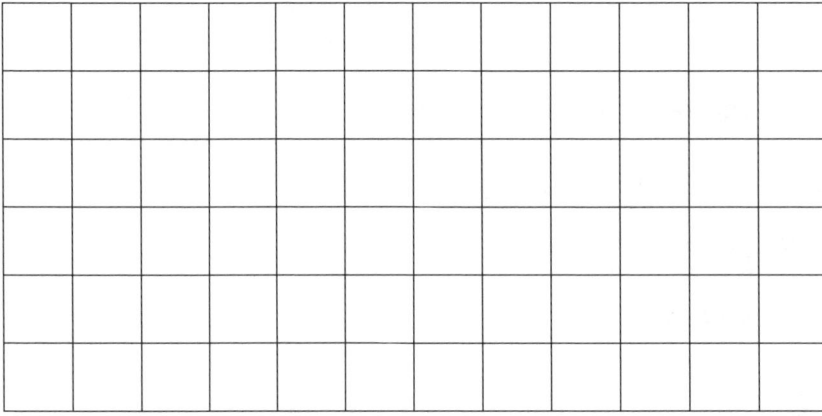

3. A square has a perimeter of 48 cm. What is the area of the square?

Perimeter = 48 cm

Area = [    ] cm²

4. A rectangle has an area of 96 cm². If one of the sides is 16 cm, what is the length of the other side? _____ cm

5. What is the area of this room?

12.5 m

6 m

_____ cm²

**6.** Draw a rectangle on this grid with an area of 24 cm².

**7.** A square has an area of 49 cm².
What is the perimeter of the square?

Area = 49 cm²
Perimeter = _____ cm

**8.** This shape has two parts, A and B. What is the area of each part?

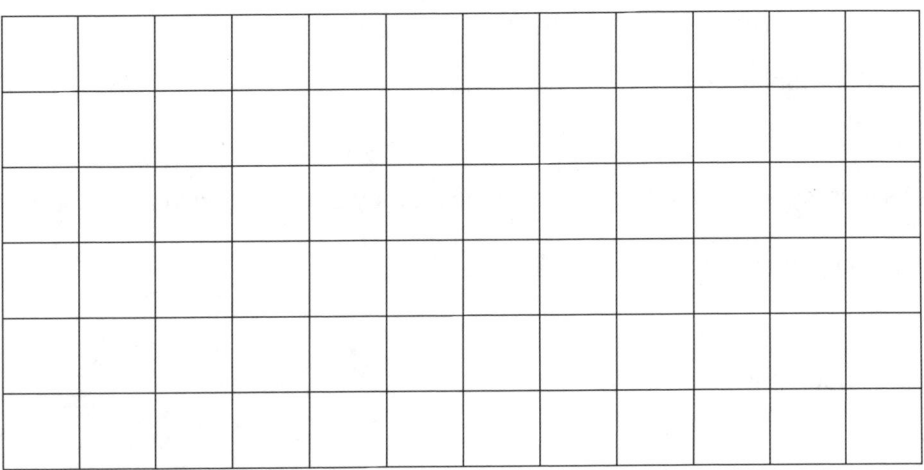

**a)** Area of A = _____ cm²

**b)** Area of B = _____ cm²

**9.** What is the total area of the shape, A + B?

Total area = _____ cm²

**10.** A rectangle has an area of 120 cm². If one of the sides is 15 cm, what is the length of the

other side? _____ cm

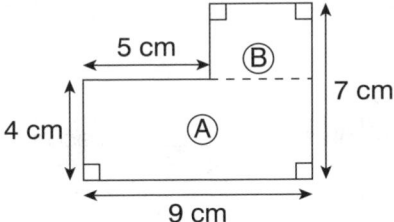

/10

1. Write these as 24-hour clock times.

   **a)** 8 o'clock in the morning → _____

   **b)** 8 o'clock in the evening → _____

2. A train starts its journey at 13:50 and completes the journey 2 hours 30 minutes later.

   What time does the journey end? _____

3. Write these as 24-hour clock times.

   **a)** a.m.

   [ : ]

   **b)** a.m.

   [ : ]

   **c)** p.m.

   [ : ]

4. Complete these:

   **a)** 1800 seconds = _____ minutes   **b)** $10\frac{1}{2}$ minutes = _____ seconds

   **c)** $8\frac{1}{2}$ hours = _____ minutes   **d)** 720 hours = _____ days

5. If the time is 11.38 a.m., what time will it be in $3\frac{1}{2}$ hours? Write your answer using a.m. or p.m.

   _____

**6.** Draw hands on the clocks to show these times.

a)
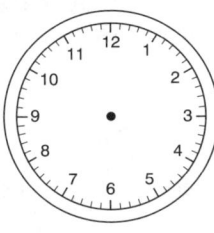

10 : 42

b)
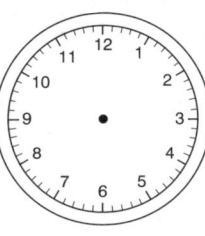

14 : 08

c)
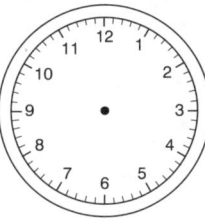

20 : 36

**7.** If today is Thursday 1st May, what date was it yesterday?

_____

**8.** Write these times using a.m. or p.m.

a) 16:45 → _____    b) 11:53 → _____    c) 23:05 → _____

**9.** A train takes 1 hour 15 minutes between each stop. Complete the timetable.

| Aston | 10:42 | | |
| Bunstone | | 15:25 | |
| Caleby | 13:12 | | 20:44 |

**10.** Write these times using the 24-hour clock.

a) 10.35 p.m. → _____    b) 8.49 a.m. → _____    c) 3.55 p.m. → _____

/10

## Probability

Use the probability scale below to decide whether these events are **impossible** or **certain**, or if they have a **poor chance**, an **even chance** or a **good chance**.

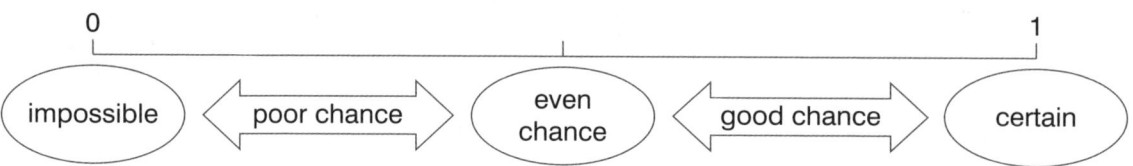

1. You will build a snowman tomorrow. _____

2. You will throw an even number on a dice. _____

3. You will eat chips this week. _____

4. The sun will rise tomorrow. _____

5. On this spinner, what is the chance of spinning a white?

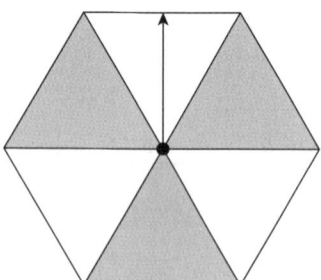

Tick the correct probability.

impossible ☐   poor chance ☐   even chance ☐   good chance ☐   certain ☐

**6.** What is the probability of rolling these on a normal 1 to 6 dice? Draw lines to match each statement to the likelihood.

| a 6 |
| an odd number |
| a number less than 7 |
| a number greater than 8 |

| impossible |
| poor chance |
| even chance |
| good chance |
| certain |

A bag contains 6 red beads, 3 blue beads and 3 green beads. Choose the correct statement for each likelihood.

impossible

poor chance

even chance

good chance

certain

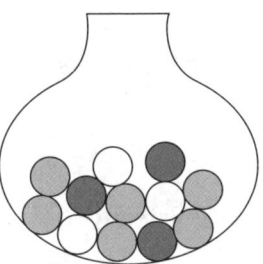

**7.** What is the likelihood of picking out a red bead? _____

**8.** What is the likelihood of picking out a green bead? _____

**9.** What is the likelihood of picking out a bead that is not blue? _____

**10.** What is the likelihood of picking out a yellow bead? _____

/10

## Tables, charts and graphs

This table shows the maths test scores of a group of children. Use the information in the bar chart to answer the questions.

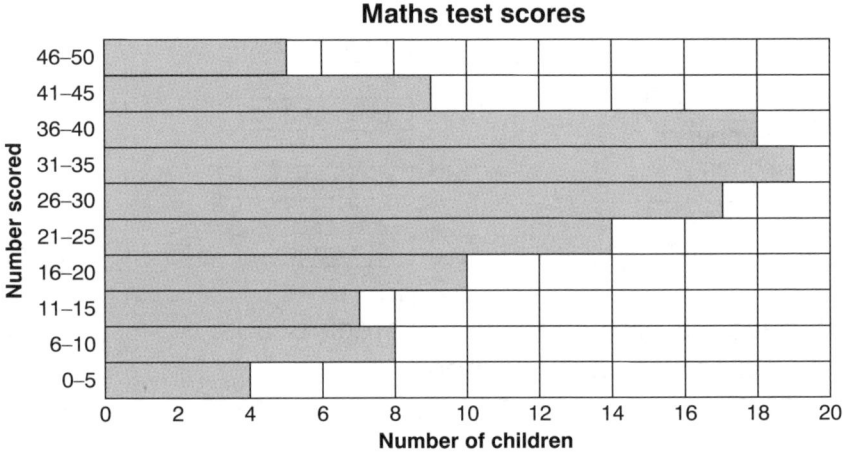

**Maths test scores**

1. How many children scored between 26 and 30 correct answers?

   _____

2. How many children scored between 46 and 50 correct answers?

   _____

3. How many children altogether scored more than 30 correct answers?

   _____

4. How many children altogether scored 20 or fewer correct answers?

   _____

5. What was the **mode** range of scores for this maths test?

   _____

This graph shows the performance of a cyclist in a race.

**Cycle race**

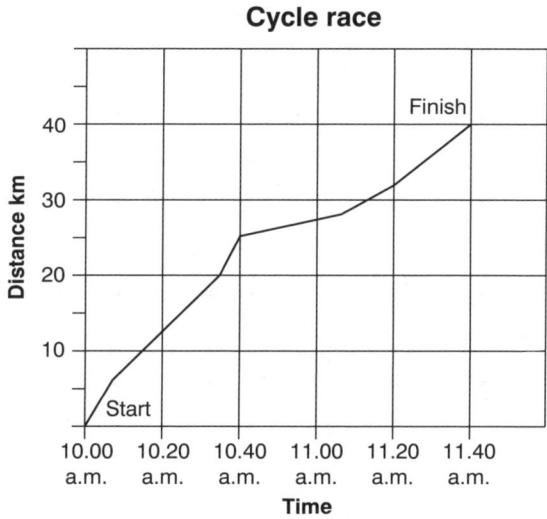

**6.** What time did the race start?

_____

**7.** How far had the cyclist travelled after 1 hour?

_____

**8.** At what time did the cyclist travel 32 kilometres?

_____

**9.** What was the length of the race?

_____

**10.** How long did it take for the cyclist to complete the race?

_____

/10

## Shape puzzle

Add one extra triangle to each shape to make it symmetrical.
Colour each shape to make symmetrical patterns.

Move horizontally or vertically one number at a time through this maze to the finish. You can only move on to a number that is a multiple or factor of the number you are on.

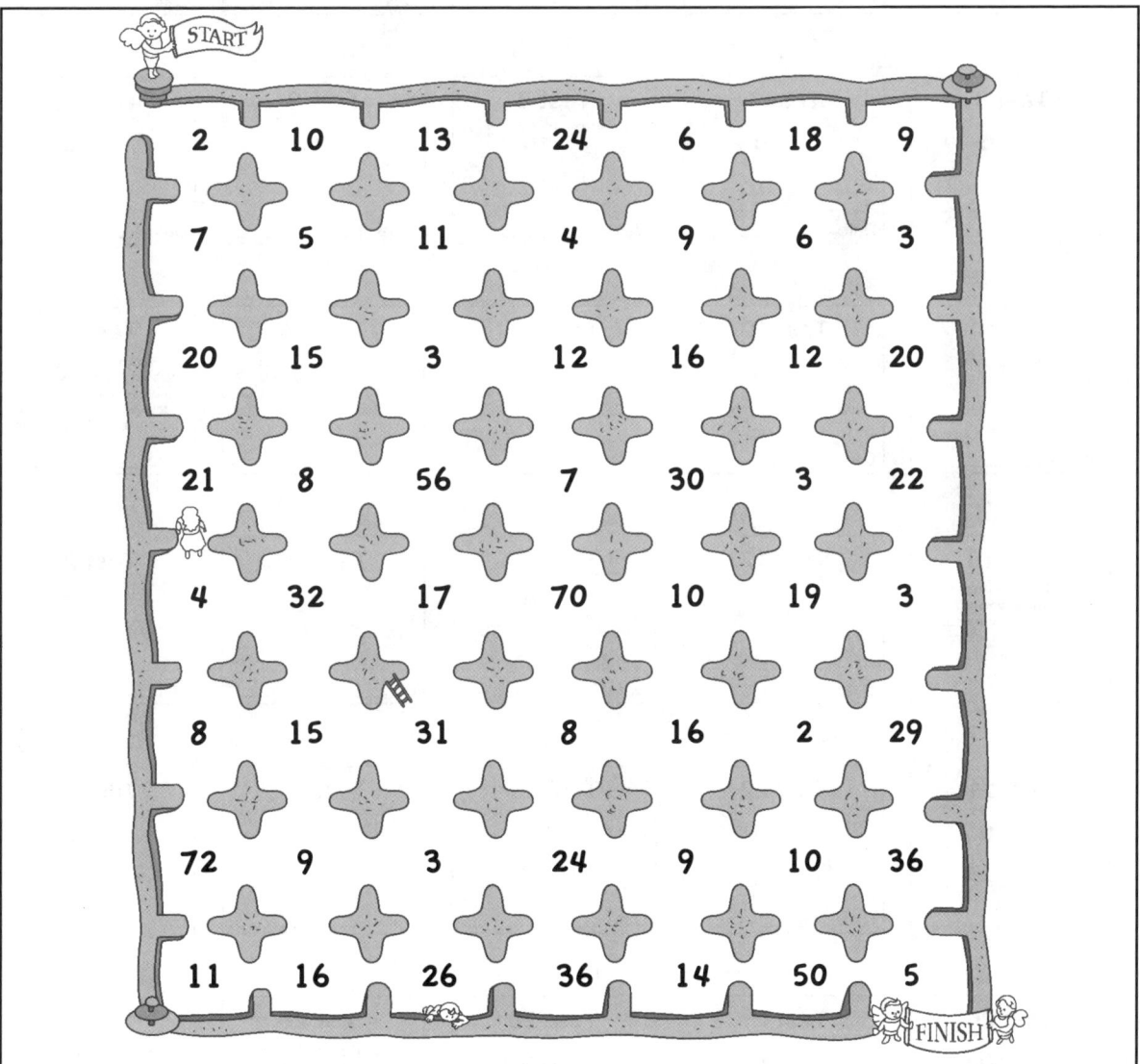

# Progress report

| | | | | |
|---|---|---|---|---|
| **Test 1**<br>/10<br><br>Date _____ | **Test 2**<br>/10<br><br>Date _____ | **Test 3**<br>/10<br><br>Date _____ | **Test 4**<br>/10<br><br>Date _____ | **Test 5**<br>/10<br><br>Date _____ |
| **Test 6**<br>/10<br><br>Date _____ | **Test 7**<br>/10<br><br>Date _____ | **Test 8**<br>/10<br><br>Date _____ | **Test 9**<br>/10<br><br>Date _____ | **Test 10**<br>/10<br><br>Date _____ |
| **Test 11**<br>/10<br><br>Date _____ | **Test 12**<br>/10<br><br>Date _____ | **Test 13**<br>/10<br><br>Date _____ | **Test 14**<br>/10<br><br>Date _____ | **Test 15**<br>If you got all of the missing numbers in less than 10 minutes, colour this red, or colour this blue if it took you longer.<br>Date _____ |
| **Test 16**<br>If you did this in less than 10 minutes, colour this square red, or colour this blue if it took you longer.<br>Date _____ | **Test 17**<br>/10<br><br>Date _____ | **Test 18**<br>/10<br><br>Date _____ | **Test 19**<br>/10<br><br>Date _____ | **Test 20**<br>/10<br><br>Date _____ |
| **Test 21**<br>/10<br><br>Date _____ | **Test 22**<br>/10<br><br>Date _____ | **Test 23**<br>/10<br><br>Date _____ | **Test 24**<br>/10<br><br>Date _____ | **Test 25**<br>/10<br><br>Date _____ |
| **Test 26**<br>/10<br><br>Date _____ | **Test 27**<br>/10<br><br>Date _____ | **Test 28**<br>/10<br><br>Date _____ | **Test 29**<br>If you complete all the shapes, then colour this square red.<br>Date _____ | **Test 30**<br>If you complete the maze, then colour this square red.<br>Date _____ |

Colour each box in the correct colour to show how many questions you got right.

0–2 = yellow, 3–5 = green, 6–7 = blue, 8–10 = red

This will help you to monitor your progress.